AN ABUNDANT LIFE

The Memoirs of Hugh B. Brown

Hugh B. Brown (ca. 1970).

AN ABUNDANT LIFE

The Memoirs of Hugh B. Brown

Edited by
EDWIN B. FIRMAGE

Foreword by
SPENCER W. KIMBALL

SIGNATURE BOOKS
SALT LAKE CITY
1988

© 1988, Signature Books, Inc.
Signature Books is a recognized trademark of Signature Books, Inc.
Printed in the United States of America
All rights reserved
96   95   94   93   92   91   90   89   6   5   4   3

Book and cover design by Smith & Clarkson

All photographs appear courtesy Zola Brown Hodson

Library of Congress Cataloging-in-Publication Data

Brown, Hugh B., 1883–1975.
    An abundant life : the memoirs of Hugh B. Brown / edited by Edwin
B. Firmage.
      p.   cm.
    Dictated memoirs, arranged and edited by Firmage.
    Includes index.
    ISBN 0-941214-61-3 (pbk.)
    1. Brown, Hugh B., 1883–1975.   2. Church of Jesus Christ of Latter-
Day Saints — Presidents — Biography.   I. Firmage, Edwin Brown.
II. Title.
BX8695.B69A3 1988
289.3′32′0924 — dc19
[B]   87–32469
                                                       CIP

TABLE OF CONTENTS

FOREWORD

Spencer W. Kimball
TWELFTH PRESIDENT OF
THE CHURCH OF JESUS CHRIST OF LATTER-DAY SAINTS
[*Edited from the eulogy delivered in December 1975;
reproduced courtesy of the Spencer W. Kimball family.*]

What a great philosopher, and what beautiful, rich philosophy he has given us! Ralph Waldo Emerson said, "It is easy in the world to live after the world's opinion. It is easy in solitude to live after one's own. But the great man is he who, in the midst of the crowd, keeps with perfect sweetness the independence of his character." Such a great man was Hugh Brown Brown.

David sang, "What is man, that thou art mindful of him? and the son of man, that thou visitest him? For thou hast made him a little lower than the angels, and hast crowned him with glory and honour. Thou madest him to have dominion over the works of thy hands; thou hast put all things under his feet" (Ps. 8:4-6). And God said, "Let us make man in our image, after our likeness . . . And God blessed them, and God said unto them, Be fruitful, and multiply, and replenish the earth, and subdue it" (Gen. 1:27-28).

This is the destiny of man; this is the work that was assigned to President Brown and to all of us: to overcome weaknesses and imperfections in self; to give parentage to other spirits; to subjugate the earth. He was one of those who, with his youth and strength, carried a high sacred light and asked for naught but chance to work, shape, and fight with strength and fortitude for the benefit of posterity.

In his early life, President Brown helped to build canals and rear dams. The water was sent running down its chiseled way; trees were planted—great spreading trees with a vision of the future. He caused horses to lean against the rustic plow. His strength and courage helped others to carry on in the building of a great commonwealth.

Men like Hugh B. Brown are not accidents. They are unqualifiedly, in the truest sense, children of destiny. If we seek their origin, we must not halt beside the humble cradle which lulled their infant cares to rest. We must rise on spirit wings above the mists and uncertainties of mortality and survey them in the light of the eternal existence, a life without beginning or end.

A friend of mine said, "Once in an age, from out of the teeming throngs of humankind that pass in swift procession across life's state, there comes a man. Not one who swiftly soars to trenchant fame and falls again unnoted and unknown, nor yet who rides in public favor and then departs forgotten and alone. But one who, thinking not of selfish greed or pining for the rabble's fickle jeers, lives but to serve, and serving, lives indeed beloved and honored through the ageless years."

President Brown lived a large part of two centuries. Few of us have that privilege. He saw great changes in this world which were part of his own. His philosophy was sound. Brother Hugh B. Brown left a great collection of classic statements, testimonies that will live forever.

Listen to what he said on marriage: "After marriage, little misunderstandings, if not talked out and thrown out, may lead to tragedy. Anything that tends to irritate, aggravate, or alienate the companions in this holy relationship should be discovered, acknowledged, and removed before real tragedy occurs. A pebble in the shoe, though very small, if not removed may irritate, fester, and even poison the foot. Thus may small irritations and disputes, if unresolved, lead to serious consequences."

He was an authority on family, for his parents had fourteen children, and he himself and his sweet wife, Zina, had a large family of their own. On expecting perfection in marriage, he said, "Neither [spouse] should ask for nor expect perfection in the other for the simple reason that he cannot give what he asks. True love is not blind, but it has the genius to magnify virtues and minimize faults when looking at the beloved." Speaking of happy marriages, he said, "When the husband and wife tell each other of their affections and demonstrate it by their conduct by both what they do and refrain from doing, then their marriage, like the tides of the ocean, will not be seriously disturbed by the surface storms. Love is a wonderful ballast. The husband lying on a couch in the front room may shout to his wife in the kitchen and say, 'Honey, I love you,' but his conduct says more loudly, 'I love me.' And pertaining to the in-laws in this marriage, which is so important to us all, as each new marriage craft sets sail, there should be a warning call which is familiar to all ocean travelers: all ashore that's going ashore. Whereby all the in-laws should get off the matrimonial boat and return at infrequent intervals and then only as invited guests for brief visits. If they are wise and polite, they will remember that they are merely guests and not members of the crew. They will make no comment on the condition or the management of the ship and will leave the controls entirely in the hands of the captain and his mate. To do otherwise is to invite trouble for hosts and guests alike."

In his first sermon after he became a member of the Council of the Twelve Apostles, he said, "My dear brethren and sisters, I respond to this call in deep humility with a keen sense of my own inadequacy, but with confidence in my brethren who have thought me worthy of it. I shall spend the balance of my life trying to make their judgment good. I could mention many to whom I am indebted as others have done. I shall not take that time. I cannot, however, refrain from speaking of my angel mother who, when I was a little child, had faith in my destiny, and all through my life helped me to believe and try to be worthy of it. I would be ungrateful if I did not acknowledge that Zina Card Brown, my beloved wife, is more responsible for my being here today than I. To these two women, I am profoundly grateful and thank God for their lives and their influences in my life."

In concluding that address, he said, "I restate my faith; I rededicate my life; I thank you for your confidence. I pray for forgiveness for my weaknesses and sins, and ask for your charity and tolerance, and for God's blessings, in the name of Jesus Christ, amen."

We loved Brother Brown as men can love each other, in honor and integrity and as a great light in our lives. We noted his family life; we have been proud of that and have taken some note of it for our own. We learned many lessons from this great man, and we say in conclusion, Remember, life is eternal. President Brown will live on for eternity. He will become, as the scripture tells us, one of the innumerable gods, and will have a world of his own and will welcome us to it.

EDITOR'S INTRODUCTION

President Hugh B. Brown, my grandfather and a General Authority of the Church of Jesus Christ of Latter-day Saints from 1953 until his death in 1975, had an intuitive sense of history. For some, such as early twentieth-century Mormon historian and church leader Brigham H. Roberts, whom Grandfather greatly admired and respected, this expressed itself in chronicling and interpreting the past. For others, like Grandfather, this sense of the historic surfaced in their appreciation of the need for future generations to understand the present.

In early 1969—stimulated by the previous year's hard-fought U.S. presidential election (Grandfather's candidate, Hubert H. Humphrey, lost), the tragic assassinations of Robert F. Kennedy and Martin Luther King, Jr., and the beginning of the end of the Vietnam War—Grandfather and I were one day discussing the portent of these and other events for the future, particularly the future of the Mormon church to which Grandfather had dedicated his life. Perhaps believing that his time was short (he was eighty-seven years old and suffering from Parkinson's syndrome), Grandfather asked that I attempt to write his biography. I enthusiastically agreed.

Using my even-then-antique reel-to-reel tape recorder, we began an oral history of Grandfather's life. These taping sessions extended through 1969 and most of 1970. Almost all of our taping sessions were conducted in his office. I prepared my questions beforehand, after sketching his life in outline. I tried to encourage Grandfather's chronological narration of his life, but periodically I would probe more analytically, hoping that he would elaborate on people and events important to his story and to our understanding of ourselves and our institutions. We proceeded, in other words, both horizontally and vertically, topically as well as chronologically.

Grandfather was a master storyteller, so much so, in fact, that I sometimes had to remind him gently to return to the subject at hand, especially when he would almost automatically begin to recount some of his best-known speeches. At these times, I would suggest, with a little needling, that the "horsefeathers are getting a bit deep" and that we should probably retrace that particular period of time or those specific events once more, this time "for real." He would invariably respond with a deep chuckle and a loving flicker of the eye that said, "You nailed me again, Eddie."

Despite the stories, Grandfather told the truth — as he remembered and believed it. He knew the purpose of the taping: that the results, in one form or another, would one day be published. He felt, like B. H. Roberts before him, that we Mormons have nothing to fear, individually and as a people, if we tell the truth.

Even so, I am sure that many intimate stories remained untold. All of us must make such a decision: what to reveal and what to keep within us. The material he chose to share with me, however, with the intent of publication, is presented in what follows. This was his request and my obligation. Grandfather loved and believed in his church as wholeheartedly as any person, and I doubt that any part of these memoirs will prove embarrassing, unless one believes that a different set of ethical principles applies to ecclesiastical office than to other institutions or to the context of individual lives. Grandfather did not believe in such a double standard and neither do I.

Some days found Grandfather more alert than others. Occasionally the effects of Parkinson's syndrome prevented our accomplishing much. If I was unsatisfied with our results, we would try again, going over the same material later.

Our taping extended over eighteen months. After completing the taping and gathering other original materials, I received an appointment in 1970–71 that took me to the United Nations in New York City and to the arms control negotiations in Geneva, Switzerland, as a United Nations Visiting Scholar. Fearing that Grandfather might not live much longer, and realizing that his presence would be invaluable to his biographer, I suggested to Grandfather that Mormon historians Richard D. Poll and Eugene E. Campbell be approached to write his biography. He agreed and to our good fortune both men said yes. I turned over to them my transcription of the tape recordings and the other materials I had gathered. They accomplished the real work of researching and writing a full, admirable biography, which was published in 1975 as *Hugh B. Brown: His Life and Thought* (Salt Lake City: Bookcraft). While information culled from the oral history occurs throughout this biography, I believe that Grandfather's own first-person reminiscences are valuable in their own right.

In what follows, Grandfather's memoirs appear almost exactly as they were dictated to me in 1969 and 1970. Some passages have been rearranged into a more chronological order, but in other instances his nostalgic detours are left unchanged. The memoirs have been edited for grammar and usage; no attempt has been made to censor any of Grandfather's candid, refreshing observations. *An Abundant Life: The Memoirs of Hugh B. Brown* is composed almost entirely of the interviews I conducted with him, although occasionally relevant letters, blessings, speeches, other interviews, and diary entries are silently introduced into the narrative.

My debt to others is deep. Charles Manley Brown, Mary Brown Firmage, and Zola Brown Hodson generously shared with me documents and photographs in their possession, as well as their own thoughts and reminiscences of their father. The family of former Mormon church president Spencer W. Kimball kindly agreed to the inclusion of President Kimball's remarks delivered at Grandfather's funeral as a foreword. At Signature Books, I appreciate the help and encouragement of Gary J. Bergera, Ron Priddis, Connie Disney, Susan Staker, Jani Fleet, and Brent Corcoran. My thanks, also, to Kedric A. Bassett for preparing the index.

I believe that Grandfather would approve of what follows and hope that through it his memory and example might continue to live on.

AN ABUNDANT LIFE

The Memoirs of Hugh B. Brown

CHAPTER 1

EARLY YEARS

I was born in Granger, Utah, west of Salt Lake City, on October 24, 1883, a second son and fifth child. At the time, my parents were living on Redwood Road, somewhere near 4800 South Street, on the old Chrissman Ranch. Later, we moved to what was known as the Lawrence Ranch, about ten miles west of Salt Lake City out beyond the old Brighton Ward where I went to school initially.

Like most, my first memories are of my father and mother, Homer Manley Brown and Lydia J. B. Brown. My father's father was Homer Brown and my mother's father was James S. Brown, neither of whom were related. (My mother did not have to change her name when she married my father.)

My father was a large man, very independent and somewhat difficult to live with. He was a stern disciplinarian, having been raised in the old school of the pioneers. It meant little to him to chastise any of his children rather severely. His own father had three wives and was also a hard, dictatorial, self-sufficient type of man. Consulting with his wife was below his dignity.

Mother, on the other hand, was kind, generous, sympathetic, and understanding. Sometimes my mother's and father's two natures clashed. But mother never stood up to father because he had a violent temper, a sharp tongue, and otherwise could be very hard to be around. Still, she was loyal to him and upheld him in many of the things he did but was heartbroken by his severe discipline and unruly temper.

Not surprisingly, the first thing I remember from my youth is my father's harsh discipline. Sometimes my older brother Homer James, named after his father and grandfather, would be slapped to the ground while working on the garden. This also happened to me a few times. My mother's heart would break a little each time it happened.

I would not want to leave the impression that my father was not a good man. He loved his family sincerely and did everything he could for us, but he disciplined us severely and wanted our prompt and immediate obedience to any of his orders. Although I admired my father and loved him in a way, I never felt intimate or close to him. Even up to the time of his death, his awful temper and quick tongue alienated practically all the members of his family from him.

The person who influenced my early life most was, of course, my mother. She seemed to feel from the beginning that I had a destiny to fulfill. I remember her telling me many times when we talked intimately that if I would "behave myself" there was nothing I could not do, become, or have. She held that promise before me all my life. Mother was a soft-spoken yet high-spirited woman of deep faith. Her father had been a member of the Mormon Battalion and had filled seventeen missions for the church—all of them after he had had one leg shot off. My mother's influence, her faith in me, and her tender feelings for all of her fourteen children—seven boys and seven girls—inspired me to be and do the best that I could. I encountered many temptations in my early life, as all young boys do, but I always thought to myself, "I cannot do this and let my mother down." In every case that I can now recall I overcame the temptation and never yielded to anything that would have in any way reflected poorly on my mother. To me she was an angel.

Next to my mother and, later, my wife, my older sister Lily had the greatest effect upon my young life. Lily was eighteen months older than I and looked upon me as her closest relative, next to our mother. Because of that trust and confidence, I went to her with most of my problems. She was something of a guardian angel to me throughout my young life, always there, pulling for me. She defended me even against my father and defied him to touch me whenever he was about to knock me down.

Another influence on my upbringing was my older brother Bud. One day Bud and I saw a weasel. The little animal ran into his hole, and we got a spade and began to dig him out. We dug down quite a ways, and Bud said, "I think I can hear him down there, we are pretty close to him. Maybe you'd better reach in and see what he's doing." I rolled up my sleeve and reached down into the hole. Well, the weasel got me by the finger, and I still have a scar.

On another occasion, Bud and I went out to the barn, where he helped me up until I could get ahold of the rafters across the top with my hands. Bud said, "I will swing you back and forth. When you get going pretty good, I will tell you when to let loose of that rafter and when to grab the next one." He gave me a good long swing and then said, "Now." I let loose of the rafter, but the other one was not within reach. It took me six hours to wake up as I landed on the back of my head. Needless to say, mother was very concerned for my welfare.

So things went on between Bud and me. But I never felt any animosity or ill-will towards him. It seemed to be part of my education, although he certainly had me in trouble most of the time. But the time soon came when I wanted to get even with Bud for all of his mischief. I had read a story in which a man died, was put in a big vault, and then came to life again. He got out of his casket in the night and walked around, trying to find his way out, but he kept placing his hands on the faces of the other dead men around him. It was a terrible, horrifying story. I knew if I could get Bud to read it he would react as I had. So I asked him to read it. As he read and marked the book I watched him carefully. When he got to the place where the man was walking around among the dead men, Bud was very excited, to say the least.

At the time, we slept on some hay in the basement of a big barn at Lake Breeze (where my father managed a fourteen-acre orchard between North Temple and 200 South streets on Redwood Road). When Bud got to this place in the book, I said, "Leave your book now and we'll go to bed." He put it down reluctantly and we went out to the barn. I pulled the barn door open. Inside was as dark as a stack of black cats. I had previously arranged for a cousin to be in the basement in a sheet. When we opened the door and he saw this ghost standing at the bottom of the steps, Bud gave an unearthly scream and started to run. I overtook him and brought him back. "That's just the result of the book you've been reading," I said. "Don't be so foolish. I'll show you there's no ghost there." I went down the steps, felt all around, and could not feel the ghost.

Bud decided to trust me. He went down, got into bed, and covered up his head, but he was shaking all over. I said, "Don't be so foolish, Bud. Uncover your head and look around you. You'll see that there are no ghosts here." He uncovered his head and the ghost was standing right at the foot of his bed. He let out another unearthly scream, covered his head again, and began to pray. I felt very guilty because he told the Lord all the bad things he had done and promised never to do any more. Finally, the ghost went away. I guess Bud's prayer had a great effect on him, as well.

When I was about fourteen years old, my father decided to move to Canada. Mother was heartbroken to give up her home, but father was determined to go. Besides what economic advantages he may have believed were to be had there for a farmer, my father had also been asked to go there on a work mission for the church to help build a canal. He left for Canada in 1898. My brother Bud went with him as did my sister Edna who had married Nathan W. Tanner. Edna and Nathan were the parents of N. Eldon Tanner, who was ordained an apostle in 1962 by President David O. McKay. Mother and the other children and I stayed behind until the others had established themselves in Canada.

When my father left with Bud, he left me in charge of the Lake Breeze ranch. As a boy I had worked with my father on the orchard, helping him to plant trees, currant bushes, shrubs, flowers, and to build a big barn behind the red brick house. I remember a hydraulic ram at the bottom of a small hill, installed by my father, which pumped water into a large tank father had purchased from the railroad. The water was piped from the large tank down into a cellar underneath the house; the pipes running back and forth made shelves for milk. Pans of milk sat on these shelves and were skimmed when the cream rose. I have vivid memories of that big cellar, which every fall was always loaded with apples, potatoes, a barrel of sauerkraut, cabbages, and beets — practically a year's supply of the necessities of life.

Although I was quite young at the time my father went to Canada, he said, "I expect you to take care of this land just as I have done." I took his words seriously and did everything in my power to make good. I think I did make good in that we raised the stock, milked seven cows morning and evening, fed the pigs, cared for the horses, did the gardening, planted the crops, and harvested the fruit. During this time, I also attended the Franklin School on Seventh South and Second West streets in Salt Lake City.

We walked to and from school in those days. It was quite a long walk from Seventh West to Redwood Road, especially in the winter when it was cold. I had to leave home with just enough time to get to school because there were so many chores to do in the morning. After school I had to run home as fast as possible to get the rest of the chores done in the evening. I did not have an opportunity to play ball, to play marbles or tops, or to engage in any of the other games that young boys enjoy because I was the man of the house and of the farm.

Later, in 1899, mother and the rest of us left for Canada to join father. We went up by train. We packed our furniture and belongings and shipped out from Salt Lake City to Lethbridge, Alberta. It was a long, tough trip that took four days. We were met in Lethbridge by father and some others with teams and wagons. We loaded the furniture and our belongings into the wagons and traveled to Spring Coulee, a little village fifteen miles east of Cardston. Spring Coulee was so named because of a bottomless spring in the coulee. It boiled up like a geyser. Our little home was built to the side of this spring.

We arrived on my birthday and found that the only provision for our family was a two-room log house. There were ten of us in the family at the time. We boys slept in tents that were pitched outside. The first winter was very cold and was a real trial to us city boys who had never had to experience anything like that in our lives. I did not have much time to think about what was going on—I was only sixteen years old then. I just did what had to be done from day to day.

One of the things I remember was that in the fall of 1900 father purchased one hundred small cattle, "dogies" they were called, that had been shipped in from eastern Canada. They had been raised on small farms and had apparently been fed pretty much on buttermilk. They were stragglers—weak, underfed, undernourished—and gave little promise. You could buy them cheap, which is why father bought a hundred of them.

Father shipped these hundred head of cattle into Spring Coulee in the fall. The day after they arrived we had one of the heaviest snow storms in the history of that part of the country. We had no place to put the cattle, no provision had been made for any shelter. We had not been able to get our hay in, and the cattle were consequently turned out on the range where they seemed to want to get as far away from their owners as possible, scattering west to the Cochran Ranch and east to what later became Magrath and Raymond.

Father took sick just after the cattle arrived and was in bed all winter. Mother was left in a log house with the children to care for. Most of the responsibility for the family fell on my shoulders. My job was to ride every day, rounding up and bringing in these scattered dogies. My companions were mostly cowboys of a rough type. It was one of the hardest winters I have ever known.

Next to the Mormon colonies in Canada was a big Indian reservation—the Blood Indian reservation, one of the largest in Canada—and our cattle got over onto the reservation. I used to ride from early morning till late at night every day, including Sunday, no matter what the weather was. It was often forty-five degrees below zero, and we would start out in the morning and have to sit in the saddle all day. Of course we were well dressed. We had heavy chaps and heavy felt boots. But it was awfully cold. Any part of the body that was exposed to weather like that would freeze almost instantly. My nose, chin, cheeks, ears, and hands all froze at least once.

Two of the men I rode with, Bill Short and Bob Wallace, were especially rough. One of them, Bill Short, was reportedly a murderer who escaped from Arizona to Canada to get away from the law. He later married my cousin Maud Brown. Bill was the best rider, bronco buster, calf roper, and bull dogger in the country. Bill had to have a part in anything that was rough and tough.

I remember riding up behind Bill once without his knowing that I was there and calling his name. He whirled around and faced me with a pistol in his hand. He said, "Don't ever do that. I may shoot you before I have time to think." He was that type of man. He made fun of me for not wishing to drink and smoke. So did Bob Wallace.

Once we went to Lethbridge with wagons to transport loads of lumber back to Spring Coulee. We got our wagons in Lethbridge in the evening and left early the next morning with four horses on each wagon. I was very young and had never handled horses or wagons, so I had to learn as I went along. After driving out to what was known as Pot Hole, the men stopped and decided to have a drink of whiskey. As they got their bottle of whiskey out, one of them carelessly dropped it on the frozen ground, and of course its contents were spilled. They then cast lots to see who would ride back to Lethbridge to get a new supply, the rest of us standing by our teams during the long trek. I resolved then that I would never become a slave to liquor.

The influence of these men on my life was negligible except that they made me more than ever determined that I did not want to follow the kind of life that had made of them the kind of men they had become. It was fortunate that I was thrown against this at an impressionable time of my own life when, because I came home every day to my mother, I was determined not to yield to temptations that beset my path.

I remember feeling at the time that I was somewhere between two futures or epochs. I was just finishing one and starting another. I never criticized my father for having purchased those cattle, given our situation at the time. I did think of it as a bit of bad judgment, but that was as far as it went in my mind. His decision would have ordinarily been a good one, but that year the storm caught us before we were ready.

We had been living in Spring Coulee for two years when father realized that he must take his family somewhere to get them in school since during those two years all of us had been out of school. We traded our land in Spring Coulee for some farms near

Cardston. We boys were old enough to take care of the farms. I was eighteen years old.

Our crops were not successful as a rule, and we had one reverse after another until all of us became thoroughly disgusted with farming operations. This resulted, as I now remember, in all of us leaving the farm, one after another, and taking up other activities.

I will always think of myself as Canadian. I have a great feeling for Canada. I remember being intrigued by the Mounties. They were glamorous with their coats and hats. Becoming a Mountie was almost at the top of my ambitions, but I never took any steps in that direction. I lived thirty years in Canada, and when I returned to the United States, it took me five years to become repatriated.

During the winter of 1903-1904, I attended the Brigham Young College in Logan, Utah, where I would take some high school work. While in Logan, I would live with Zina Young Card, the daughter of Brigham Young and wife of Charles Ora Card, the founder of Cardston, whom my family had come to know in Canada. Aunt Zina was the mother of my future wife, although it was not until later that I realized that this would be so.

Shortly after arriving in Cardston, my mother and I attended a wedding party of some kind. Aunt Zina, who was living in Cardston at the time, had brought her little daughter Zina along with her to the party. Zina was only thirteen years old but gave a recitation. She had golden curls down to her shoulders and had a delicate, wistful look upon her face. As I looked upon her I had the indelible impression that she would one day be my wife. I told my mother about it as we sat in the room. I said, "I am going to marry that girl some day." Mother said, "I hope you will. She is a wonderful girl."

After my family and I arrived in Canada in 1899 and found ourselves isolated on a farm fifteen miles from the nearest school house, I realized that if I was ever going to amount to anything I must make it myself. Therefore I soon obtained some books and began to read. The books that I remember most were the Bible, first, and the Book of Mormon and the Doctrine and Covenants.

8

I became well acquainted with all of them. I was sixteen years old when I began my study of the scriptures.

I knew that I had to go on a church mission some day and I wanted to be prepared so I studied everything that I could find. I remember a little book called *Reminiscences of a Mormon Missionary*. This book had a great effect on my life because it told of a man who was in similar circumstances to those in which I found myself. I read it constantly. I was a voracious reader from then on.

The two books I remember best in those early days, in addition to the scriptures, were *The Secret of Achievement* and *When a Man's a Man*. These two books, with which I lived during those lonesome days in Spring Coulee, were read by lamplight in the tent when it was often many degrees below zero. I would put on a fur coat and a fur cap and sit up at night and read.

Besides *The Secret of Achievement*, the other book that I think touched me most deeply was *Architects of Fate*, both of which were written by Orison Swett Marden. These books appealed to young men to make the best of their opportunities, and while I thought I did not have much opportunity, I was determined that I was going to prepare myself for future usefulness. Later on, of course, when I was in Cardston I obtained other books and read as often as I could—books like *Lives of Illustrious Men*, *The Struggle of Religion and Truth*, and especially Harry Emerson Fosdick's books, *The Meaning of Faith*, *The Meaning of Prayer*, and *The Meaning of Service*.

I also had some ambition for social life, knew some girls, took some out to dances, and so on. But never during all this time did I become intimate with any girl. Never once did I do anything that now, as an old man, I look back upon with regret. This I attribute to my mother's influence.

While at Spring Coulee, we lived on a road down which all the visitors to the Alberta Stake had to pass at the time. They had to pass by our farm and ordinarily stayed at our place over night. This is how I met Francis M. Lyman, Heber J. Grant, President Joseph F. Smith, and many other leaders of the church. One to whom I was especially attracted was Apostle Orson F. Whitney. He was a great poet and a magnetic speaker.

9

I looked upon these apostles with almost worshipful feelings and wondered if ever I would be able to be familiar with any of them. At that time I did not anticipate what lay ahead, but I do remember that I thought if there was any way in the world to prepare myself for such a high calling, I was going to do it. With this in mind I devoted myself assiduously to getting an education and improving myself to make up for the loss of opportunity for earlier training in school.

My first memory of church leaders dates from 1893. This was before we went to Canada, when my mother took me and some of the other children to the dedication of the Salt Lake Temple. President Wilford Woodruff was in charge of the dedicatory services. All of the General Authorities were present. I remember looking at them, especially at President Woodruff, and wondering how he got to be the kind of man he was.

My mother later purchased for me a copy of the *Life of Wilford Woodruff*, by Mathias F. Cowley. I learned that President Woodruff was a man of the farm, that he had very little education, but that he was a man of great faith. Anyone who came close enough to him to shake hands with him was impressed by his deep spirituality. He seemed to be a man who talked with God. I held him up as an ideal for myself. Incidentally, he was also a great friend of my father. They had farms that adjoined each other in Salt Lake County in earlier days.

The next man that touched my life deeply was President Joseph F. Smith. In 1901 he became the president of the church upon the death of Lorenzo Snow, who had succeeded Wilford Woodruff. Joseph F. Smith looked like a prophet. He had a long beard, an attractive countenance, and a bearing proud and stately. He sat and talked to us in our home whenever he went from Lethbridge to Cardston by coach. Joseph F. Smith touched my life very deeply.

He once took occasion to talk to my three older brothers and me about his early life. He told us he had gone on a mission to Hawaii when he was only fourteen years old. He told us of the struggles he had had, of his lack of educational opportunities, and of his gradual growth. He told us of an incident in his own life when he had had to depend upon God and his prayers had been answered in a miraculous way. I looked upon him as a man who truly was a servant of the Lord. He became another ideal in my life.

Of course, all men are human beings, and I learned later in life that even the General Authorities are subject to certain faults and failings.

President Smith was, in a way, a very rugged man who had been raised in the school of hard knocks. I remember, later in life, finding out that he could be very severe in his judgment and very exacting in his demands upon his family. But unlike my father, President Smith was also a man who was loved deeply by his family. He had several wives and was very just and fair in his dealings with them. In the days of Brigham Young, with whom he had associated, the man of the house was expected to be severe and was respected for being such.

In some ways Joseph F. Smith seemed to me to be a man that I would like to have had for my father, but I knew if he had been my father his severe discipline would have been hard on me. President Smith's discipline was different from my own father's, but such behavior seemed necessary in those early days. The thing that impressed me most was his prophetic calling. He seemed to carry with him an aura of deep devotion, and when we heard him pray at night, as he did, we knew that he was talking with God. At those times I would think in my soul, I hope someday I can talk with God as this man does.

Because of my father's attitude toward my mother and President Smith's attitude toward his families, I made up my mind early that I would govern my own family by love and not by force. I attribute this determination, which I have followed throughout my life, to the fact that I knew men who were great and good men but who, it seemed to me, kept their families in awe and did not get close to them. I made up my mind when I married and had children that I was going to try to get close to each of them, as my mother had done with each of us.

I think I have succeeded fairly well in this, although there are many things I remember now, as I look back over the past, that I would like to have changed a bit. For example, I think I left too much to my lovely wife to do. I left her with many duties with which I could have helped her if I had been thoughtful enough. But, all in all, I think our family was raised in a spirit of love, for which my wife was more responsible than I.

All of the discipline in our family depended upon me, and I had enough of father in me to exercise control. Still, in all our married life, raising eight children, I do not remember once having to give any of them a whipping. I sometimes thumped them on the head with my fingers, corrected them sternly, but I never found it necessary to use physical force, and I never did believe in whipping children. It would have broken my wife's heart if I had.

Zina and I never had any quarrels in our lifetime, at least none that I can remember. She was a sweet, gentle spirit. Even if I believed that whatever I said was the law and testimony, we still never had any violent disagreements. Of course we had the usual problems to face, and we tried to face them together. She has stood side by side with me through good and bad weather.

I do not hold myself up as an ideal, or as perfect, in any respect. Everyone has troubles in raising a family during the early years of their marriage and the teenage years of their children. And, like others, we had the usual amount of that. But I think we feel grateful now, as we look back and remember, that our children have nothing to regret that either of their parents went too far astray. They knew when I told them they had to do something, that they had to do it. I never had very much trouble getting any of them to feel this way. And I do not remember any of my children at any time willfully disobeying my orders.

I became a stake president quite early in my life; I had previously been a bishop's counselor and was in the high council before that. I remember saying more than once to my own children, as did their mother, "Remember who you are," or "You must do so and so because your father is well known." I think now that this was probably not a good thing for them. They may have felt that they were not individuals in their own right and may have looked upon me as someone removed from them because I was thirty-seven years old when I was made a stake president. Since that time they have only known me as President Brown. I am sorry

to say that I have seen the effect of my possibly overbearing attitude in the lives of some of my children, that they have sometimes been overly timid, fearful, pessimistic, and even depressed.
I now regret this very much.

Of course, each child is different, and we have to treat them
all alike by treating them differently. Some of them have been
more active in the church through the years than others. Most
have been quite active, holding positions in wards, stakes, and
even on a general level. But one daughter did not want to take
any part in the church at all and has kept pretty well aloof from
it. From the time she was a little girl, she resented my position
and seemed to feel that I was robbing her of her birthright by not
giving her enough time.

In 1904, I came down to Salt Lake City from Cardston to go
on a mission for the church to England. As I left Cardston on the
train my mother was at the station to tell me goodbye. She said
to me, "My boy, you are going a long ways away now and you
will be on your own. Do you remember when you were a little
boy you often had bad dreams? Do you remember that you would
cry out in the night? Your bedroom was next to mine and you
would say, 'Mother, are you there?' And I would say, 'Yes, son,
I'm here, just turn over and go to sleep.' You always did that,
knowing that I was near and that you didn't need to fear any
more. Now, I'll not be there when you arrive in England, more
than five thousand miles away, across a continent and an ocean,
but if you will remember God is as close to you as you will let
him be, and if when any emergency arises, you will call out and
say, 'Father, are you there?' there will come into your heart a feeling of his presence, and you will know that you have someone
upon whom you can depend."

Many, many times since then, in the ensuing sixty or more
years, I have cried out and asked, "Father, are you there?" And
always I have had the impression that he was mindful of me, was
available to me, and would see me safely through.

When, at the beginning of my mission, I went through the
Salt Lake Temple, I met Heber J. Grant and he later helped to set
me apart as a missionary. I had earlier met Elder Grant, who was

13

a member of the Council of the Twelve Apostles, in Spring Coulee and in Cardston, and I believed that I knew the man pretty well.

When I arrived in England, Elder Grant was the president of the European missions, including the British mission. He treated me very kindly. I looked upon him as a great and marvelous man. But here too there was evidence of clay in the feet of the great, for I found him to be self-opinionated. He had been successful in finance but had also had many setbacks and had had to fight his way through.

I remember one incident in 1905 that was impressed upon my mind after I had been in the mission nearly one year. I had kidney stones. The pain was so severe that the local English doctors told me I must go home and have medical attention or I would die. President Grant learned of this and made a special trip from Liverpool to Norwich to tell me that I would be released and sent home. This broke my heart.

I said to him, "President Grant, if you will give me a blessing, I will not have to go home. I will get well."

"If you have the faith that that is so," he replied, "it will be done." He then blessed me and I did not have another attack of kidney stones.

This experience tied us together. He remembered it, as did I. He even mentioned it once before he died. He said, "I remember that when you were a young man you had faith that if I gave you a blessing you would go home without having to submit to any operation or medical care."

As the years passed, every time I crossed the path of Heber J. Grant I felt that I was in the midst of greatness. He seemed to have a special feeling toward me and told me once that he expected great things of me. He seemed to take up the story where my mother left off. He was a great speaker in his own right. One of the General Authorities once said that he was the greatest orator in the church. I heard many of his stories time and time again, but he had a style of speaking that made it impressive even though I knew what he was going to say.

I later learned that he did not have a son, only daughters, and that this was a great source of sorrow to him. He seemed to want

14

to adopt me in a way. In fact, when Aunt Zina, my mother-in-law, went to him after I had spoken to her about marrying her daughter, he said, "Zina, I have seven daughters of marriageable age. Hugh Brown can have any one of them he wants. That's my answer to you as to whether or not you should let your daughter Zina marry him."

President Grant and I thus seemed to share a tender feeling towards each other that lasted until his death in 1945. He was responsible for my being made a stake president both in Canada and later in Salt Lake City. I attribute much of my tenacity of purpose to the stories he told of how the things we persist in doing become easier to do. His stories left a lasting impression upon my mind.

Many of the people who knew President Grant thought of him chiefly as a financial man. They did not look upon him as a prophet like Joseph F. Smith. I was one of these. I thought he was a great leader, but I did not feel the same towards him as I did towards President Smith.

Later, in 1937, when I was called to preside over the British Mission, President Grant asked me to accompany him to the mission field. We traveled all over Europe together. For five weeks I was in his presence daily and sometimes during the night as we occupied the same hotel rooms. I learned to love the man and to know something of his deeper nature. This is perhaps best illustrated by an incident.

We were on a train going from town to town, holding meetings where we could, and were pulling into Heidelberg, Germany. As the train slowed down, about to stop at the railway station, we looked out the window and saw a huge crowd of people. As the train stopped we let the window down and the people broke into singing "We Thank Thee, O God, For a Prophet." They were singing in German, of course, but we knew the tune.

President Grant arose and put his head out of the window. Tears rolled down his cheeks as he looked upon those people. The train only stopped a few minutes before we pulled out again. When he sat down beside me he was still crying.

"Hugh," he said, "I am not entitled to that kind of adulation. This is what they used to do for Brigham Young when he traveled from Salt Lake City to St. George. To think they would feel that way toward me and to sing 'We Thank Thee, O God, For a Prophet,' and be referring to me . . . I am not entitled to this."

While he was talking he put his head in his hands and his elbows on his knees and went on talking. I thought he was talking to me for a time, but I discovered shortly that he was talking to God. Then he said, "O, Father, thou knowest that I am not worthy of this position, but I know that I can be made worthy, and I want to be worthy. I want thy spirit to guide me in all that I do and say." This, to me, showed the spirit of the man. Great humility, great faith, although he had weaknesses which at times seemed to overcome these admirable qualities.

President Grant was a tenacious businessman. In banking, in insurance, in the sugar company, and in other ways, he showed his ability as a businessman, but much of his success resulted from his tenacity to put over a deal which, in many instances, I think, could be rather sharp. That was one of his great weaknesses—one that made it difficult for some people to support him. But I learned, and knew from the time I went to preside over the British Mission, that in addition to his financial ability, he was a prophet of God and lived very close to the Lord.

Prior to my presiding over the British Mission, in 1927, I came to Salt Lake City to practice law. When I came down from Canada a question in my mind was whether I should be a Democrat or a Republican. I spoke to several people about it. President Grant at the time was an ardent Democrat, as was his counselor and cousin, Anthony W. Ivins, and B. H. Roberts. Each of these men told me at different times and separately that if I wanted to belong to a party that represented the common people I should become a Democrat but that if I wanted to be popular and have the adulation of others and be in touch with the wealth of the nation, I should become a Republican.

I took what these men said seriously and became a Democrat and have stayed a Democrat, even though President Grant later turned very bitter towards Franklin D. Roosevelt because he thought he was dishonest. President Ivins remained true to the

Democratic party, as did B. H. Roberts, Stephen L Richards, and other men and women of those times. I never found a reason why I should change my own political allegiance.

Later, President Grant wanted me to do what he had done and join the Republicans and forget the Democrats; he was rather pronounced in his denunciation of the Democrats as a whole. I had the affrontery to tell him that I thought he had turned his back completely on his own allegiance and that he should have stayed a Democrat. We argued on this point quite a bit as we traveled over Europe. At that time he was just making his complete change of allegiance politically and his cousin, Anthony W. Ivins, pleaded with him to stay true to the party.

B. H. Roberts was, of course, another outstanding Democrat. Because of this, he was sometimes out of harmony with many of the other brethren, but he had the temerity to stand up for what he believed in and to suffer for it. I knew him well and was impressed with his ability as a speaker, a writer, and a leader. In my opinion, he was the greatest defender of the church we had had up to that time. He and Orson Pratt were the two that I looked upon as the main ones who built a case for the church which could not be gainsaid. One of the greatest speeches he ever delivered was his discourse to the congressional committee which was deciding whether he, as a polygamist, should retain his seat in congress during the 1890s. He rose to great heights on that occasion. I traveled with B. H. Roberts on many occasions. He became my ideal so far as public speaking was concerned and contributed much to my own knowledge of the gospel and to my own methods of presenting it. I owe a lot to B. H. Roberts.

I remember B. H. Roberts and John Henry Smith, who at the time was a counselor in the First Presidency, entering more than once into a powerful battle on politics. You see, John Henry Smith was an ardent Republican. On one occasion, B. H. Roberts told John Henry Smith that he should wash his mouth out with soap because of the things he had said about the Democrats. John Henry replied, "I'll wash my mouth out after you have taken some lye to your own mouth and cleansed from it some of the terrible things that the Democratic party is guilty of." This was a battle

royal between two giants. I thought that B. H. Roberts came off
victorious, but, of course, my thinking on this is prejudiced.

More than ever, as I think back on the years since 1927 when
I returned to the United States, I would still choose to be a Democrat rather than a Republican. I realize that by that choice I would
be in the minority — almost a minority of one — among the General Authorities, since most of them are now Republicans. But
my conversion to the principles of the Democratic party has been
complete, and as time goes on I become more and more convinced that the Democrats have the right philosophy, both as to
their foreign policy, their progressiveness, and as to their refusal
to look back or to stand still. Theirs is the party of progress. I do
not want to give a political speech, but I am more of a Democrat
now than I ever was.

Another of the great men of the church was John W. Taylor,
the son of church president John Taylor. He was a prophet and
often made predictions that I lived to see fulfilled. For instance,
he once stood on the hill where the temple now stands in
Cardston, Alberta, at a time when there was just a handful of
Saints there and said, "The time will come when a temple will
stand on this hill. At that time, you will be able to take your breakfast in Cardston and your dinner in Salt Lake City." That seemed
like an impossible thing because it then took three days to get
from Cardston to Salt Lake City.

I was present when he made other predictions, as well. He
predicted the success of the Cardston Saints' farming operations
when, because of early frost, or late spring, or for some other
reason, it looked as though the crops would fail. He told them to
go ahead. We once harvested the best crop we ever had in Canada after a big hail storm when it looked as though all was lost.
John W. Taylor was a powerful speaker. He moved the people.
He did a lot of good. I respected him for his life and for his devotion, but I could not agree with his support of polygamy after
the Manifesto. He was, of course, excommunicated for his practices and was only recently reinstated.

Of those who had the greatest impact on my life, I think most
immediately of Joseph F. Smith, John W. Taylor, and Heber J.
Grant. But I would also like to mention someone who was not a

member of the General Authorites but a bishop of a ward in Cardston. I was his counselor, was just twenty-five years old, and had just been married.

At this time, Bishop Harris was forty-five years old, and we two counselors were full of fire and needed some lessons in humility, tolerance, charity, and love. A young woman, accused of sin, was brought before us. She confessed her sin and tearfully asked for forgiveness. Bishop Harris asked her to retire to another room while we considered our verdict.

He then turned to us. "Brethren, what do you think we should do?"

"I move we cut her off from the church," the first counselor said.

"I second the motion," I added.

Bishop Harris then took a long breath and said, "Brethren, there is one thing for which I am profoundly grateful, and that is that God is an old man. I would hate to be judged by you young fellows. I am not going to vote with you to cut her off from the church. I am going out and get her and bring her back. The worth of souls is great in the sight of the Lord."

We did not agree with him at the time but subsequently learned that he was right. Some fifty years later I was back in Canada to hold a conference. Sitting on the stand I noticed in the audience a woman whose face had many lines and some rather deep wrinkles. Her face showed a life of hardship, struggle, but was nonetheless the kind of face that engendered faith. I asked the president of the stake who that woman was and he told me. I went up to her and she told me who she was before she had married. She was the girl the other counselor and I had wanted to cut off from the chruch.

Afterwards, I asked the president what kind of a woman she was. "She is the best woman in the stake," he said. "She has been a stake president of the Relief Society and a ward Relief Society president. She sent four sons on missions after her husband died. She has been faithful and true all the days of her life."

Of course, the president did not know what I knew about her, but his praise confirmed to my mind this truth: the Lord wants us to have charity and love and tolerance for our fellow men. If we forgive others, including ourselves, the Lord will for-give us. There is no reason we should hold against our fellow men any of their transgressions. This is a lesson I have learned repeatedly throughout my life and one I hope I will never forget.

CHAPTER 2

MISSION AND COURTSHIP

From 1904 to 1906, I served the church as a missionary to England. One of the most memorable of my experiences there occurred in Cambridge, my first assignment upon arriving in the British Isles.

When the president of what was then called a conference (now a district) sent me to Cambridge, he said that my companion would be Elder Downs, an older man whose mission had ended. He explained that Elder Downs would go with me to Cambridge, help me find lodging, start me tracting, after which he would leave for France on a tour.

The president then added, as if what he had to say did not matter much, "You may be interested to know, Elder Brown, that the last Mormon missionaries in Cambridge were driven out by a mob at the point of a gun and that they were told that the next Mormon missionaries who stepped foot in the city would be shot on sight. As you are the next missionary who is going to set foot in that city, I thought you might be interested in this." Of course, I was.

After arriving in Cambridge, Elder Downs and I found that word of our coming had preceded us. Near the platform of the station, where we arrived, were many billboards reading, "The rascals are returning." One of the signs in particular made an impression on me. It was a picture of a man with a long beard holding an ax over a woman lying prostrate at his feet, her head on a block. Underneath her, the sign read, "Will you go into polygamy or won't you?" This gives an idea of the bitterness that existed in Cambridge at the time.

We eventually found a place to stay. Elder Downs told me how to mark my tracts and that was all. He left the next morning. I learned later that there were no LDS members within many

21

miles of Cambridge. I felt very lonely. However, I did go tracting. I was wholly unsuccessful the first day, a Friday. I tracted all morning without one invitation or conversation. I tracted all afternoon with the same results. I was very depressed.

Saturday morning I went out again and tracted all morning without any apparent results. I came home, and in my heart I felt a mistake had been made in sending me there—in fact, in sending me on a mission at all—as I did not seem to be able to make any impression upon the people.

As I was sitting alone in my little room that Saturday evening I heard a knock on the door. The landlady answered and I heard a man say, "Is there an Elder Brown living here?" Of course, I thought that this was the advance guard of a mob, and I was terribly agitated. The landlady replied, "Yes, come in."

He came into my room holding a tract and said, as he looked at me, since I was a raw cowboy type of lad, "Are *you* Elder Brown?" I more than understood his amazement at finding so young and apparently incapable a man representing a church, but when I told him I was, he said, "Did you leave this tract at my door this afternoon?" Since my name was on it, I could not deny it and answered, "Yes."

"Elder Brown," he continued, "last Sunday a group of us in the Church of England left the church because we could not agree with our minister. He was not teaching what we believe to be the gospel. There were seventeen of us heads of families who were out of harmony with the minister, and we told him we would not return. We all assembled in my home. I have a large home with a large hall-like front room which accommodated us and our families. Will you come tomorrow night and be our pastor?"

He told me of their having prayed through the week that before the next Sunday the Lord would send them a new pastor. He concluded, "We know now that our prayers have been answered."

I said what any Mormon missionary would have said: I told him that I would come. But after he left I could not help but wonder what I was up against. I had not been in the mission field three days. I had never attended a meeting in the mission field. I had never spoken before an audience in the mission field. I felt terribly weak and incapable.

I worried about it all night. I went to bed without supper. I went up to my room, prepared for bed, knelt at the side of my bed, and for the first time in my life I actually talked with God. I told him of my predicament, of the challenge that lay ahead of me, of my inadequacy, of my lack of training and knowledge, and I asked for help. I seemed to get no reply. I got back into bed, lay for some time, and got out again and renewed my prayer for help. This went on most of the night.

The next morning I advised the landlady that I would not desire any breakfast, and I went for a walk. I walked up to the university buildings, wandered around the campus, and felt terribly lonely and forlorn. I came in at noon to tell her I would not want any lunch, and I went back and walked again all afternoon. I seemed to have had a short-circuited mind. I did not seem to prepare or to try to prepare what I might say, but going through my mind was simply the thought, "You are to be the pastor of these people who are seeking the truth. How are you going to do it?"

When I finally returned that night, it was Sunday, and as I sat by the fire contemplating the mission that was before me, I felt despondent and blue, indeed. Finally, the time came when I had to go. At a quarter to seven I arose and put on my Prince Albert coat and my stiff hat, both of which were foreign to me. I suppose I looked rather peculiar in that kind of an outfit as I had so recently come from the range. I took my walking cane, put the Bible under my arm, and started for the house. I dragged myself down the road. In fact, I think I only made one track all the way.

Upon arriving, and before entering the gate, the man of the house came out onto the porch. He bowed politely and said, "Welcome, Reverend Sir, come in." I had never been called a reverend before and that frightened me and made me feel very much out of place. But we went into the house and found the large room completely filled with people. They stood out of respect for their new pastor and that scared me, too. Not until that moment did I realize that the whole of the evening would depend on me, that I had to do the praying, the preaching, and, as it turned out, the singing. Not knowing anything else to do I said, "Let's sing 'O, My Father,' " the Mormon hymn by Eliza R. Snow. They looked at me with a blank stare, but we sang it. It was a terrible cowboy solo. I was much embarrassed.

Thinking that I would be less ill at ease if they knelt and took their eyes off me, I suggested to them that they turn around and kneel at their chairs while we offered the opening prayer. I knelt with them, and at that very moment every bit of worry and concern and doubt and question left my mind.

After the prayer, I started to talk to those people, wisely doing away with the second hymn. I talked for forty-five minutes. More accurately, the Lord spoke to those people. For while I prayed to him at the beginning of the meeting, I said, "These people are seeking for the truth. We have that truth, but I am not able to give it to them without thy help. Wilt thou take over and speak to these people through thy holy spirit and let them know the message of truth."

I spoke, as I said, for forty-five minutes. At the end of the meeting, after closing the services, the people came around me with outstretched hands; many of them, with tears in their eyes, said, "This is the gospel we have been asking for. This is the message we wanted our minister to give us, but he would not. Why couldn't we have had it before?" They were so delighted with what had been said that they indicated a desire for us to meet again.

I mentioned earlier that I had to drag myself to that house. On my return home that night, it seemed to me that I only touched the ground once, so elated was I that the Lord had come to my assistance.

Within three months every man, woman, and child in that room had been baptized Mormons. This was not my fault; I had little to do with it. I was simply the conduit through which the spirit worked, touching the hearts of these people and making them realize the truth of the gospel. I believe that most of them remained true to the church the balance of their lives. Practically all of them subsequently emigrated to the United States. I saw many of them at various times, and they referred always to that wonderful occasion of what to me seemed to be almost a day of

Pentecost. I continued on my labors as a missionary and was assigned to labor in various cities in the Norwich district. My later successes compared favorably to those attending the efforts of the other missionaries. But I'll never forget Cambridge.

I would like to introduce at this point a second experience, one showing how I had changed and grown since I addressed that little group of men and women in the building in Cambridge. Shortly before the time arrived for me to come home, there was a local preacher in one of the other conferences who had given an elder there a lot of trouble and who was constantly challenging him to a debate. Finally, he sent his challenge to President Heber J. Grant of the British mission who forwarded the preacher's letter to me. The preacher's letter read simply, "Send me the best man you have in your mission and I will debate with him and defeat him." To be honest, I was elated with the prospect of such an encounter, as I had considerable faith in my ability to meet with such a man.

On my way to the debate, I thought, "I can lick that fellow with the scriptures I now have at my command." Much to my surprise, as I now think about it, I did just that. This man spoke first; I afterwards, occupying almost an hour in teaching the first principles of the gospel and the restoration.

At the close of the meeting, the man said, "I have been opposing you Mormons all along, but I want you to know now that what I have heard tonight has convinced me that I was wrong and that you are right. I want to join your church."

He did join the church, and I was very proud of what I had accomplished, but I did not realize at the time that I had accomplished it without the aid of the spirit that helped me at the time of the beginning of my mission, and that later troubled me.

My greatest trial as a missionary occurred in Cambridge, just a few weeks after the experience that I related above. We were staying at a home where a widow and her two daughters lived. One of the daughters was about eighteen years old; the other was about twenty years old. They were both very attractive. The widow seemed to be quite determined that her daughter should marry a Mormon elder. She was not a member but was very much impressed with our teachings and finally did become a member.

This woman told me at one time I should have Laura, the younger of the two sisters. I was not interested and made no attempt to become familiar with her. However, when one of my companions left for a trip to France, I was suddenly alone again in Cambridge. On this occasion, this young lady came into my room at about two o'clock in the morning, clad only in a short chemise, and said to me, "Would you like to have a bed fellow?"

I thought for a moment of what my mother had said and of what my sister Lily had said. I thought of their entire confidence in me. I thought of what would happen if I should yield to the blandishments of this young woman. I sat up in bed and commanded her to leave the room immediately and not come back. I was very abrupt in what I said, and she left rather hurriedly. That was the moment of decision for me on my mission. Many times thereafter young ladies made approaches, and I had many opportunities where I might have yielded and had a good time with them, and perhaps even committed sin, but after that experience in Cambridge there was no thought in my mind of anything but to be true to my calling.

A highlight of my mission was when President Joseph F. Smith came over to visit the British and European missions. He and President Grant were holding special mission conferences in London and we were invited to go and to meet with them. I was elated with the thought that we would be able to come into contact with the president of the church.

I have never before or since, I think, experienced the feeling that came over me as I sat and listened to these two men speak. I was a young, inexperienced, untrained man, but somehow I knew in my heart that what they said was true, and I thought at the time how wonderful it would be if by righteous living I could come to a point were I would be in a companionship with such men, little knowing what lay ahead of me. That was the highlight of my entire mission so far as the teaching of the gospel is concerned.

Near the end of my mission I was laboring in Norwich. I had been tracting, and at that time we went three times to every door, regardless the reception. On this day I came to a door where I remembered the woman had been particularly antagonistic. I knocked on the door with the big brass knocker. I knocked as a mature missionary knocks, for I had been in England nearly two years. New missionaries sometimes knock rather carefully hoping they will not be heard. But I knocked vigorously and had no response.

I looked through the window and saw a woman sitting in the front room knitting. I recognized her, for she had given me a tongue lashing before, and I knew she was neither deaf nor dumb. She would not respond so I went around to the back door. In those days we carried a walking stick. I took my walking stick and knocked on the door so hard that she came out like a setting hen comes off the nest in response to a troublesome boy.

For several minutes she gave me the worst Scotch blessing I have ever had. But she had an impediment of speech and had to stop every few minutes to draw her breath.

When she did stop, I said, "My dear lady, I apologize for having annoyed you, but our Heavenly Father sent me 6,000 miles to bring you a message and inasmuch as he sent me I can't go home until I give you that message."

"Do you mean the Lord sent a message to me?" she asked.

"I mean just that," I answered. "He sent it because he loves you."

"Tell me the message."

And I told her as best I could the Joseph Smith story. She listened intently, apparently impressed.

Then I again apologized for having been rude enough to insist on her coming out and added, "Sister, when you and I meet again, and we will meet again, you are going to say, 'Thank you, and thank God that you came to my back door and insisted on speaking to me.' "

Ten years later, in 1916, I was in England again, this time in uniform. President George F. Richards was the president of the mission. He had the flu, and he called me at the military camp and asked if it was possible to get a leave and go down to Norwich to hold a conference for him. I, of course, was very glad to visit my old mission field. At the close of the morning session a woman and four grown daughters came down the aisle.

I was shaking hands with old friends, and as I took her by the hand she bowed her head and kissed my hand and wet it with her tears. She said, "I do thank God that you came to my door ten years ago. When you left that day I thought about what you had said. I couldn't get it out of my mind. I was fighting it, but I couldn't sleep that night. I kept thinking, 'God has sent a message to me.' But," she said, "I fought it for three days. I tried to find the missionaries from the address on the tract you left, and when I found them, you had returned to Canada. We continued to investigate until my daughter and I joined the church, and next month we are leaving for Utah."

The joy that can come into the heart of a man or a woman who has been instrumental in the hands of God in carrying the message of life and salvation to some soul, be it only one, is a joy beyond anything that men in the world can know.

During my mission the Manifesto of 1890 was often discussed in connection with the subject of polygamy, which was thrown at the missionaries all the time. It was during this time, namely from 1904 to 1906, that the United States Senate was trying the case of Utah senator Reed Smoot who had been elected a member of the senate in 1903. The question the senate was trying to answer was whether the church had been sincere in abandoning the practice of polygamy or whether it had just been a front. We were often accused of being hypocrites.

At this time, President Joseph F. Smith was called before the examining committee of the senate. He gave evidence and defended himself in a remarkable manner, I think. He was asked if all the members of the Twelve agreed with what he said was intended when the Manifesto was issued. He replied that if they did not agree they would not continue as members of the Twelve. They then mentioned two apostles—John W. Taylor and Mathias F. Cowley—who, it was known, were in Canada, and insisted that President Smith bring them to Washington, D.C., to be witnesses. President Smith replied that he had no jurisdiction outside the United States and could not command those men to come to Washington. Later, however, the Quorum of the Twelve and the First Presidency decided that these men, both of whom had refused to concur in the opinion of the majority of the Twelve to abandon the practice of polygamy, should be dropped from their positions in the quorum. Eventually, Brother Taylor was excommunicated and Brother Cowley was forbidden to exercise his priesthood in any respect or to speak in public at any time. Brother Cowley was an exceptional man, humble, tractable, but on this occasion he thought he was right. Brother Taylor rebelled against the decision of the Twelve, fought them openly, and was only then excommunicated.

George F. Richards and David O. McKay were the two men chosen to fill the vacancies caused by the dropping of Elders Taylor and Cowley. I remember having to constantly fight the idea of polygamy and its continued practice and to insist with those with whom we talked that the church was in full accord with the wishes of the U.S. government and was very sincere in abandoning the present practice of polygamy. Still, many people thought the Manifesto applied only to church members living inside the United States. Accordingly, in 1904, after he had testified before the senate committee and just as I was leaving for my mission, President Smith issued what has become known as the Second Manifesto. In that, he said, in effect, "This applies to all members of the church wherever they may live, in the United States or outside of it, and from now on any person who engages in the practice of plural marriage will, upon proof of guilt, be excommunicated."

This pronouncement had a very definite effect upon the opinions of the press and other media and resulted in a better feeling between our church and nonmembers. At that time, the *Salt Lake Tribune* was a vile and wicked periodical which attacked the church in almost every issue. It especially leveled its venom on President Smith. But he, being the prophet he was, withstood it and came out victorious.

I cannot recall much of the impact the Manifesto must have had on members of my family and others before my mission, but afterwards Brothers Taylor and Cowley made a determined effort in Canada to get as many of the brethren there as possible to enter into the practice of polygamy. Quite a number yielded to their persuasions, including the president of the Alberta Stake and the president of the Taylor Stake. As a matter of fact, these two apostles, especially Brother Taylor, were very close to my father and tried to persuade him to enter into the principle. My father steadfastly refused but, I am sure, was nonetheless affected somewhat by the logic of their arguments. Because of the firm stand of my mother and of some other members of the family, and because of what he knew to be right, my father refused to enter.

Brother Taylor then centered his attack on me. I was a young man, had recently returned from my mission, and had not yet married. He told me I might as well marry two or three women at the same time. I withstood him, and at no time since have I ever had any inclination to have more than one wife. Brother Taylor's arguments were that the word of God could not be countermanded by a law of the land, that polygamous practices came as a revelation to the prophet Joseph Smith, and that the revelation had never been rescinded or denied. He refused to accept the Manifesto of 1890 as a revelation and thought it rather to be a cowardly submission on the part of President Wilford Woodruff to the demands of the anti-Mormons throughout the country.

I remember that quite a number of the men entered into polygamy after that. Each of them came to a sad end. Most finally were excommunicated. Some repented, in which case they had to give up some of their families, which was very embarrassing to them. The whole story was rather active in our communities in Canada. We were living at this time in Cardston, Alberta. Many of the people who disapproved of the action taken by the General Authorities and confirmed in General Conference in 1904 and who hoped to practice polygamy outside the United States had come to Canada and to Mexico.

In conjunction with this, it may be interesting to note that, besides Elders John W. Taylor and Mathias F. Cowley, both a son of President Smith and a son of President Woodruff were among those who did not approve of the suspension of polygamy. Abraham O. Woodruff and Hyrum Smith, together with George Teasdale and possibly a few others of the Twelve, interpreted the Manifesto as having reference only to those residing in the United States, but Elders Hyrum Smith and Abraham

Woodruff both died rather suddenly in Mexico, if I remember correctly, one of them in a drowning accident. I do not remember how Elder Teasdale's case turned out.

As to the two local Canadian stake presidents who yielded to the persuasions of Elder Taylor and Cowley, their cases were considered carefully by the Council of the Twelve Apostles, which thought it would be unjust and improper to punish them for having yielded to the near commands of two members of their quorum. Neither man was handled for his membership in the church as a result but continued as presidents of stakes for sometime afterward. Other local leaders were notified that if they did not repent and forsake their habits they would be excommunicated. Several of them forsook their habits, gave up the practice of polygamy, and were permitted to continue, but those who did not were excommunicated. These men cared for their families, for the most part, but in some cases the unfortunate women who had become plural wives had to find their own way in life. They were not widows, they were not married women, but they had a number of children. Theirs was a pitiful lot.

I do not know of any temple sealings having been honored or performed after the Manifesto, although there may have been a few. Some marriages, I understand, were performed in Mexico, and I know that some were performed in Canada. An attempt was sometimes made to include these later sealings among those that had taken place prior to the Manifesto, as though they had been in a temple ceremony, but such was not the case. In each case, these marriages, as I understand it, were performed by one of those whose names I mentioned above and who were members of the Council of the Twelve Apostles.

After my mission I came to know Reed Smoot, whose seat in the U.S. Senate had been so strongly contested during the early years of the twentieth century. I used to play golf with him a lot, although I never did have a very close personal relationship with him. He was quite a fearless man. He was not a polygamist and eventually did win his case in the Senate, holding his seat for some thirty-seven years. He was a great representative of the people of Utah and of the church.

Reed Smoot was defeated in the 1930s by Elbert Thomas. He could not believe that his own people had turned him down. It was a terrible shock to him, and I do not know that he ever really overcame the impact during his lifetime. He continued to serve the church as a member of the Twelve and visited many stakes, but after a short while he seemed to lose his memory and was not effective thereafter. He did not, however, at any time to my knowledge deny his testimony of the divinity of the work of which he had testified throughout his life. I talked to him on the golf course shortly before his death in 1941.

"I know that what has happened to me is not the result of my church or my standing in the church," he said, "but because of some astute politicians who through the years have determined to get me and now it seems some members of the church (since Brother Thomas was then a member of the General Board of the Sunday School) have seemed to turn against me. For sometime I held it against them, but I think now I understand that it was the usual course of political activity, and that I had served the time that I was expected to serve."

As I have already mentioned, my first contact with the young woman who I decided would become my wife, Zina Young Card, occurred when she was thirteen years old and when I was eighteen years old. Later, during my years in England, I wrote to Zina occasionally, and she to me, usually addressing her as "Dear Sister Zina" and she addressing me as "Dear Brother Hugh." Three of my letters to her follow:

Cambridge
Aug 1/05

My Dear Sister Zina: —
Your welcome letter of the 13th ult. almost made me wish I were in Logan but it had such a spirit of "good times" that I could not get homesick for I felt that I was there with you. Perhaps I had better not say how I felt after I had read it and started to think of the six thousand miles which lay between us. Using Elder West's expression, I felt "all over in spots."

I am very pleased that you have had such a "fine" time this summer and I hope it may continue. How I would enjoy a good old waltz or two-step, but if I will just be patient for fifteen or sixteen months I guess I can begin to think of such things, but in the meantime I am enjoying myself immensely only in another line. I do enjoy missionary work and my whole desire is that I may do my duty.

The Lord has greatly blessed me with friends here and I am thankful that I have been instrumental in bringing some to investigate the truth. I often wish that more of our sisters could have the opportunity of doing missionary work in the world, but I suppose their work, which is great, is nearer home.

I am called to leave Cambridge next week so my address will be changed. I am not sure yet where I will be sent, but I think I will be in Norwich. As that is the headquarters of the conference, they will forward my mail to me wherever I go. We all meet there Aug 8 and will be appointed to our fields. I am glad to leave here for *one* reason but I fear if I tell you what it is you will think me vain. But I will plead "not guilty" to the charge and risk the consequence of telling you my secrets, for you know we menfolk must have a lady friend to help us keep our secrets and as you are my only lady correspondent it falls to your lot. By this time no doubt you are saying what is the kid trying to get at; well, I'll tell you.

A young lady, daughter of the lady with whom we board, went to Utah some time ago and is married to my old companion Elder Downs. As she has two younger sisters here (18 & 20) she has written back to them of the glories of dear old Utah. As they are both working for a living, which is up hill life in England, they have been suddenly (?) seized with the gathering spirit and of course they don't feel like they could undertake the trip alone so Elder West and I have been chosen by them as escorts when we get our releases. So I am glad that I will be moved soon, not that I am afraid of accepting the proposition or that I would accept it if I stayed, but it may avoid some unpleasant tasks. Elder West says he guesses he will have to face the music, but he can't treat them cold for it is unbearably hot in England. Ha! Ha! don't think me foolish for these are plain facts foolishly told. A missionary should not write this way but we are engaged in preaching the gospel so much of our time that a little change is as good as a rest.

Well, I have occupied enough of your time for one letter, but as it is all nonsense I will write more news next time.

I hope you will be successful in your schooling. As to which would be best for you to follow of the two courses you mentioned it would be hard to decide but I think you are especially gifted as an elocutionist, but you are the best judge on those matters and I know you will make a success of whatever you undertake.

Give my love to your folks and all friends and accept a large portion for "old time's sake."

Your Devoted Brother
Hugh B. Brown

I will send you a photo when I get a good one taken and would be very pleased with one of you. I have that small one of you and Bessie in my watch but I haven't got one of you alone.

Lovingly —
Hugh

★ ★ ★ ★ ★

Norwich Eng.
May 17/06

My Dear Zina: —
All alone tonight so I will chase loneliness away with my pen and try to imagine I am talking to you. Since Elder Webb left I feel like a lost sheep and "my only refuge is my pen." Don't smile, for really it is possible for a Brown to feel blue, but I am O.K. and thank the Lord I am permitted to be here.

Well, my trip to London was simply immense; and the Tout concert "superb." Those girls are certainly gifted of the Lord. I think Nannie sang before the queen again on the 15th Inst.

Nannie, Maggie and Grace are very sociable with the elders. I felt "right at home" in their company and they are not ashamed of being "Mormons" and to allow those with whom they associate to know it whether of high or low degree. I do admire true courage. I'll have to tell you all about London when I see you. I visited most of the places of interest but my visits were brief as time was limited. I hope you will have the privilege of seeing the metropolis some day for it is indeed a great place, but these good old English people are very slow, if they had the life of Chicago, London would indeed be a "seething mass of humanity."

I am glad you are going to Cardston this summer. I would like to attend your cooking class as a few lessons would be beneficial to me when I start my bachelor's home, but possibly your course will extend into the winter months, if so I may be able to join the class when I return. Ha! Ha! Perhaps it will be "ladies only" but you know I attended some of the girls' classes in the B.Y.C. and enjoyed myself just fine in spite of my bashfulness.

When you see Joseph just tell him I would like to hear from him if he *is* married. Perhaps he will not consider me in his circle until I follow suit. Well my intentions are good for the future, for a mission certainly converts a man to a few of the higher principles of the Gospel.

I have been made clerk of the conference since Elder Webb left, which is a little additional work.

Well bye, bye for this time with love to all the folks, yourself included.

I am as ever Yours,
Hugh B. Brown

★ ★ ★ ★ ★

Ipswich, England
Sept. 11 — 06

Dear Zina —

As my health has been failing for some time past, it has been deemed wisdom for me to spend this month visiting in the different branches of the conference, and especially the towns on or near the coast, so I am now in my old field, Ipswich, where I was laboring one year ago, and already I feel the effect of the bracing sea breezes which blow over the city. I will not do any tracting this month but will spend my time as a re-al-tired gent, trying to grow fat as I have lost thirty pounds in weight since xmas so you can imagine what I look like (a lamp post minus the lamp).

I am very pleased that you had such a nice visit "up home" and now I wish you could spend a month here on the coast with "mother" as chaperone. I'm sure we would have a "hot time" (it was 91° in the shade last week).

I rec'd a letter from Joseph a few days ago; he seems to be very happy, and proud of his little family, and I think he should be. He says I am "behind the times," but there are some brighter days coming, I hope.

I saw Pres. Grant last week and he said the church sends the Canadian elders direct to their homes via eastern Canada so I guess I will miss my visit in Salt Lake or at least postpone it for a time. Elder Webb and I had decided to have a gay time in S.L.C. when I returned but it seems to be another case of "air castles."

Oh, say; Victor S. Amussen, one of Joseph's old chums from Logan, is laboring in this conference. He is a fine missionary, and wishes to be remembered to you. He and I will hold meetings together next Sunday.

Eleven of us "Canucks" had our pictures taken in Bradford while attending conference there July 22 and 23. It was indeed a great treat to see so many of the home boys, I could almost feel the "chinook" and see the waving grass. We also had a very enjoyable time in London on the 26th Ult. where we went to meet Pres. Joseph F. Smith. I also met the two Nibley girls there and I tell you the Utah girls look good to me. I dreamed the night before meeting them that you were there with "Nan" and when the younger girls came in I thought sure my dream had come true. She resembles you so much. I thought for a while that I had palpitation of the heart but it was only going "pity me."

I had thought of going to Paris this month but I think I must give it up as it is a very rough trip across the North Sea and sea sickness is very common with me lately without the voyage but perhaps I will be able to do some traveling before I go home, at least I hope so. Perhaps a little chafing dish cooking would do me good, Do you think so?

Well, Zina, it is now nearly two years since I left home. It does not seem possible that I have been here so long, but I have kept quite busy and have been very happy, so that accounts for the time passing so fast. I hope to be able to go to school when I return, and then go on another mission if it is the will of the Lord.

I sincerely hope to have the pleasure of meeting you before long; if your "serious thoughts" are put into execution perhaps it will be by invitation, if it doesn't happen before I return.

Don't think from what I have said that I am sick, I am just a little "off," as you will conclude when you read this letter, but I will endeavor to do better next time.

> With love and best wishes I am
> Your Devoted Friend
> Hugh   XX one for the baby.
> Ha. Ha.

We continued like this for more than two years, until it was time for me to return home and take up new challenges.

CHAPTER 3

MARRIAGE AND WORLD WAR I

Upon my return from England in late 1906 I developed a bad case of typhoid fever and was laid up for several weeks. Before leaving for England, I had been going with a young lady for about two years. There had never been anything serious between us, and while in England I decided to break things off before returning home because I was sure she was not the girl I wanted. However, during the typhoid attack she came to my house and nursed me.

Following my illness, I went to report on my mission to E. J. Wood, president of the Alberta stake and one of the finest men I have known—he had a great impact and influence on my life. I attribute to him many of the methods I have since employed in presiding in stake and other offices in the church and in shaping the lives of those whom, because of my position, I was able to touch and influence. President Wood was a prophet in a very real sense, but because he was also a polygamist, he did not go beyond the position of president of a stake. Had it not been for that I think he would have been one of the general church leaders.

During my report, President Wood asked me if I was going to marry.

"No," I answered, "I lost my girl while I was gone."

"Who was she?" he wondered.

"Zina Card."

"I promise you now," he continued, "that if you will go to Salt Lake City immediately and tell her of your love, she will marry you."

"But, Brother Wood," I responded, "she is already engaged to be married to a man in Logan."

"It doesn't make any difference. If you will go down there and tell her of your love, she will marry you."

I believed him implicitly, as I had seen on previous occasions evidence of his prophetic power, and of course I was glad to believe it. I took him at his word and left for Salt Lake City shortly thereafter.

When I arrived in the city I met Zina's mother first. She wanted to know why I was in Salt Lake. I told her I had come to get her daughter.

"You can't have her," she said. "I don't want her to go back to Canada. I went through so much in that country. I don't want my daughter to put up with what I had to put up with. I don't want you to marry my daughter."

I told her that if she would just remain neutral I would take my chances with the battle. I then went up to see Zina.

Although I had never told her of my love, I think Zina may have been aware of my feelings. Nearly five years had elapsed since the time I had decided she was to be my wife, but I never breathed a word of it to her or to anyone but my mother until I was in the mission field, when I mentioned it to my companion George Webb. I told him I was going to marry Zina Young Card when I got home. He came home ahead of me, went to see Zina, and told her he had come to see the girl Hugh Brown was going to marry. She, of course, was shocked since she was already engaged at the time and said that she did not know anything about that, that she had always thought of me as a big brother.

When I finally saw her I told her of my true purpose and she told me of her engagement. I told her that I knew she was to be my wife and that she would break up with this other man. She said she would let me know later. I returned home to Canada a little disappointedly. But when I returned to Salt Lake City for the next General Conference of the church, I saw her again and she told me that she had broken up with her man. Still, she did not promise to marry me. I kept writing and coming back, and she finally consented to marry me in June 1908, much to my delight.

During these two years after my mission and before my marriage, I corresponded regularly with Zina while I was in Canada and she was in Salt Lake City. Four of my letters to her during this period follow:

Cardston, Alta
Canada
Dec 10—06

My Dear Sister,

No doubt you have thought that the excitement of home-coming has made me forget that I had received some letters and that I had a "sister" in Salt Lake but I assure you such is not the case for my mind has been at "No. 146" more since my arrival than ever before but on account of sickness I have been unable to write.

Perhaps you have heard from Joseph that I was taken down with typhoid fever just a few days after my arrival. Through the blessings of the Lord and the administration of the elders I had it in a very mild form, the fever was rebuked by Pres. Wood and I improved from that moment and I am very thankful to be out of bed so soon. Living on "milk only" is a little "too thin" at least it made me very "thin."

I was very pleased to get your letter of Oct. 15. It was forwarded to me from England. I received it while I was in bed with the fever and it did me more good than all of the doctor's visits and medicine. You know a little "mind medicine" and "sunshine" very often do more good in a case of sickness than the skilled treatment of an M.D.

Yes, Zina, I would have given most anything to have returned via Salt Lake, but my illness was the chief cause of the direct journey home and I just arrived in time to avoid sickness away from home, so once more that which seemed to be a trial was all for the best and I must await the coming of spring before I can have the pleasure of seeing you once more. It will be three years in April since we parted at Logan and I hope I will not have to wait longer than that before seeing you for I have the same feelings for you now that I had then only it has deepened with time and separation.

I was glad to hear that the elders called on you; Elder Webb and I were companions for some time and learned to love each other almost as David and Jonathan did.

My missionary labors were a great pleasure to me and when it is the will of the Lord I will be glad to go again. The saddest part of my mission was when I left the field. I parted with many warm friends and friendship that is formed under the inspiration of the spirit of God is warm indeed and only those who have had a similar experience know how hard it is to part with those whom you never expect to meet again in mortality, even though one is returning to his "own."

I have seen Joseph and Leona several times since my return. They are quite well and seem to be very happy. I think them almost an ideal couple but it is hard for me to realize that Joseph is really married and the father of such a fine boy.

I hope that my home coming will not stop the "letters coming" as I am always pleased to hear from you.

With love to yourself and mother I am as ever

Sincerely yours,
Hugh

★ ★ ★ ★ ★

Cardston, Alta.
Apr. 27 — 07

My Dear Zina; —

Yes, I am in Canada once more. How strange it all seems, but, when I step out in the blizzard that is sweeping over this country, I cannot doubt that it is "Canada." It has been snowing and blowing here for several days and looks more like xmas than spring.

We had a pleasant journey but it got rather tiresome before it was over, and then to get such a cold reception, — Well, it made me "Long to breath the mountain air."

We were delayed in Beaver Canyon several hours which was very tiresome to the women and children (and they were many) but I spent the time fishing with a cord and pin hook and caught — a cold.

Oh, say, it is amusing to listen to the questions I have to answer when I venture down town. It's all about the "English girl" and my future; several have been kind enough to wish me "much joy." I fear I have left a wrong impression with some of them but why should they know that which is such a puzzle to

42

me? Viz. Who is she going to be. I believe there is but One who knows, although another, with His assistance, may decide.

I saw Joseph, Leona, and Stirling [Zina's siblings] today. They were all well and very pleased with the presents your mother sent. Little Joseph is looking well and as sweet as ever; they all seem very happy. Whenever I go into Joseph's house I have "visions of the future" or "day dreams." Ha, Ha!

Well, Zina, I feel lonesome already, almost blue. I don't know what I will do before July. It looks so far off and then there is nothing certain about your coming, but I still live in hopes and feast on the memories of "What hath been."

I have not yet seen Zina W. but if the weather continues as it is I cannot go to Kimball so may see her tomorrow and deliver your message, but I remember now that you did not give me the "parcel" for her so I cannot deliver it (worse luck). You must send it in a letter.

I am not entirely over the effects of my journey and my thoughts are like the train, slow and unsteady, so I will close anxiously awaiting a letter from you.

Please give my love to all your folks and accept the same, I am as ever

> Your Loving Friend,
> Hugh
>
> S.W.A.K.

★ ★ ★ ★ ★

> Cardston, Alta.
> May 19—1907

Dear Zina: —

It has been raining quite hard all day but we had a fine conference and the house was filled beyond its seating capacity.

I have just returned from meeting and feel fine, but the day will not be quite complete without writing a few lines to the one I wish was here.

I had been watching the mail very anxiously for some time when the "female" arrived with a letter from the girl I love and I was indeed very pleased to hear from her. Yes, Zina, many times I have wished myself back in Salt Lake where we could resume our quiet strolls up the canyon, and where I could enjoy your company. Still I am happy and I believe I am in the proper place.

The time seemed so short in Salt Lake that it now seems like a dream when I think of the good times I had. How I would like to stand on the little bridge on Fourth St. tonight with you as we stood the night I left; but why wish for that which is impossible? Better hope to see you soon in Cardston for that is quite possible and I hope probable.

We had a stake officers meeting Friday night and enjoyed a spiritual feast and Saturday night the Y.L.M.I.A. gave a social party in the hall. About 10 p.m. "we young folks" left and went to the Band Hall and enjoyed ourselves in a dance; this was the first party I have attended since I came back. I had a good time but it seems rather unnatural for man to be alone. I am now christened "Bachelor Brown" since the people have found out that I really didn't get married.

I have seen Zina several times since I came home but have not been where I could deliver that message. She wanted to know what it was the other day but I prefer to wait until I can "do it right."

I am sorry to hear that Lyle feels as he does and I trust that your friendship will not be broke, but "friendship sometimes turns to love but love to friendship never."

Milton and I have some good times in the store; we are kept quite busy as a rule but we find time to joke a little and torment the girls. They "get even" with me by teasing me about "the little English girl." Well, maybe they will see her someday.

I see Leona and Joseph quite often. They are quite well or were yesterday. I didn't get to speak to them today as it was so crowded.

Mother sends love to you and your folks. She might be down in June. I hope she will and bring you back with her for I am longing for that trip to the lakes.

I must close now with love and best wishes. I am as ever yours devotedly

Hugh

★ ★ ★ ★ ★

Cardston, Alta
May "17th" 08

My Darling Zina: —

This is the 17th of May, just one month 'till your wedding day. Then how happy we will be; "*one*" for life and eternity. Beloved, although the Sabbath is a very busy day for me, I think of you the whole day thru and especially has it been so to-day the 17th.

I expect to leave here between the first and ninth, if all goes well as the rates include those dates. I think Stirling's wife will go down and we are trying to get him in the notion. They are quite well. I spent the evening there Saturday, "Shakespeare club," and of course I had several questions to answer and a little blushing to do.

Stirling's little boy came in the store and called me "uncle Hugh," to the amusement of the clerks, and then I had to make some explanations but I will soon get used to it.

I really believe I am "growing old" for I can now manage to keep a serious face all during meeting even when mice are playing 'round my feet and amusing the congregation. So, my dear, you must prepare to play the part of David and cheer the "old man" up, but you will not need a harp, your presence will bring sunshine to my soul.

The sad news reached us this evening of the sudden death of Bro. Sylvester Low Sr. I have not heard the particulars but I think it was the result of a stroke which he received this afternoon. Death is so sad. My sympathy goes out to the bereaved. How hard it must be for your cousin and uncle. I hope they will be comforted.

I hope to receive a letter from you tomorrow for your dear letters make me very happy but soon I will be by your side.

Father and Mother send love and greetings. They would have written to you before now but father has been and is quite sick. But we hope he will soon be well. The measles have left us and the children are all well. Your name is very familar in our home now and the boys all think a great deal of their new sister.

Good night, sweetheart, it's time for the "last car." Love to your mother and Rega and my heart's true affection for you. I am

Lovingly yours,
Hugh

One month later to the day after writing this last letter, Zina and I were married in the Salt Lake Temple by President Joseph F. Smith. No man ever had a truer wife, a better companion, nor was there ever a better mother in the world than my wife, Zina Young Card Brown.

After we were married, Zina and I returned to Canada. Zina's mother accompanied us, as did John Talmage, a son of James E. Talmage, who wanted to visit some relatives. Our honeymoon was not the kind that is usually anticipated by an enthusiastic young couple.

My brothers Homer, Scott, Lawrence, Owen, and Gerald met us at the train station in a little town east of Cardston, as the train at that time did not go to Cardston. They had brought with them an old rattle-trap of a buggy, an old, broken down horse, and a harness made partly out of baling wire and rope. We looked like the tail-end of nothing when we finally arrived in Cardston.

Once home, however, we were delighted to find a fine span of black mares and a new rubber-tired buggy awaiting us. This was a gift from my brothers. It was a real treat. I have never felt so proud of any automobile I have since had as I was of that pair of black mares and little buggy.

At that time I had just been made president of the co-op in Cardston. It was a large store; I had worked there for some time and President Wood had asked me to take the management of it. We sold everything from toothpicks to threshing machines — everything that people needed in that kind of country. We had a big business. But I was only getting $75 a month — not much to start on, especially since I had no capital. We moved into a small house that belonged to Charley Burt, bought some second-hand furniture, and set up housekeeping. Later, we moved into part of my mother's big home and then into the home of Telitha Carlson, where our daughter Zina Lydia was born on July 21, 1909, at 2:30 a.m. I wrote in my diary at the time:

> Zina gave birth to a beautiful girl and now I am the proud father. The Lord has blessed me with one of the best women on earth and these 13 months of married life have been a foretaste of heaven in which my joy is now crowned by the arrival of an important spirit clothed in a beautiful tabernacle of flesh of our own offering. All honor be to the Father of Spirits and may he aid us to so live that we may be worthy guardians of others and in faith fully discharge the sacred duty of parenthood.

Incidentally, I paid $2,250 for that little home. I had no money with which to make a down payment, so I borrowed from my friends—five dollars, ten dollars, twenty dollars each. We were very proud of it. It was a little home without any modern accommodations. There was no inside plumbing, for instance. We had a large pail instead of a real bath. The water was outside and we had a pump. It was very humble, but we were very happy.

Upon the birth of our first daughter, we were, I think, the happiest young couple in the world. Zina was the most beautiful child I had ever seen. Her complexion, her features, her verve for life, her long curls, everything endeared her to us beyond anything we had known theretofore. But when she was eighteen months old she was suddenly stricken with polio. I picked her up one day and her leg went limp. We took her immediately to a doctor who said, "She will never walk. That leg will not grow." It was a very heavy blow to all of us. We brought her to Salt Lake in 1914 and had a special operation performed on her foot. She has been lame all her life but could at least walk. She has made good in spite of it all and has never complained. She is now the mother of two lovely daughters and has been a special blessing to us during her own mother's recent illness.

I worked in a Cardston co-op for about two years, from 1908 to 1910, when the Brown brothers bought a thousand acres of land on the old Cochran ranch. We already had some land near Cardston, but the Cochran ranch had been acquired by the church and was being sold to members of the church, with payments extending over a long period of time. We moved out on the ranch about twelve miles north of Cardston across from the Blood Indian reservation.

We had a lot of experiences on that old ranch. Breaking the sod was quite a job. The sod was so heavy it took six horses to pull a single plow and then it had to be broken up by a disk plow to make a seed bed. But when the seed was finally planted there was no land anywhere in the world as rich. The heavy black loam in some cases was four feet deep and the crops were magnificent when we could get them. However, we unfortunately encountered one failure after another — early and late frost, heavy snows, hail storms, everything that could possibly happen seemed to happen to us. We borrowed from year to year enough money to plant another crop and we did not have a successful crop for the next four years. My brother Owen and I were the only married men at the time, and the other boys lived out there with us. Zina and my brother's wife, Ida, helped with the cooking.

We lived in a little building that had been built as a granary. There were two or three other buildings like this one, and they accommodated everyone who stayed there. During this time, two other daughters were born: Zola, on 12 April 1911, and LaJune, on 27 June 1914. Following the birth of my second daughter, I wrote in my diary:

> On the twelfth day of April my beloved wife gave birth to another lovely daughter to be companion to Zina. She is another fair-haired treasure. . . . Zola Grace is by the grace of God the second of his wonderful gifts to us in our happy married life and may they both live to fulfill the mission of womanhood as completely as their mother is doing.

Three years later, I added:

> My wife gave birth to another girl [LaJune], a beautiful body and lovely bright spirit. We rather expected a boy, but no disappointment was felt as she comes as an additional ray of sunshine into our happy home. We thank the Lord for the spirit of love and peace which has been with us in our married life and these bright jewels bind us together as nothing else could.

Our place on the Cochran ranch was a lovely farm, but we could not make it because of the successive total crop failures.

Father had gone to that country to make sure that we boys would be independent and not have to work for somebody else for our wages. But father was not with us very much; his health was failing and he did not spend much time on the ranch. He and the rest of his family were living in Cardston. My sisters joined us on the farm when they could be helpful.

Initially, the farm was badly run down and overrun with weeds. The shrubs and trees, too, had been seriously neglected. One morning, as I went out, I saw a currant bush and noticed that it had grown up all out of proportion. In fact, it had gone to wood; there was no sign of either blossom or fruit. Having had some experience on my father's fruit farm in Salt Lake City, I knew a little about pruning. So I decided to prune this currant bush. As if to set the bush's mind at ease, I said to it, as I took the shears in hand, "Someday, when you are laden with currants you will thank me for cutting you down so that you could grow properly and develop the fruit that you were created to produce." I have since had occasion to reflect back upon that afternoon and have had applied to me my own words to the currant bush.

Despite our best efforts, we were never able to make a real living on the farm, so we finally gave up and I started to work with my wife's brother, Joseph Card, in the insurance and real estate business. This was around 1913 or 1914 when many people were asking if the Latter-day Saints would participate in preparing for what some said was the inevitable war to come.

At this time the Dominion government at Ottawa had passed a law known as the Militia Act creating what is comparable to the National Guard in the United States. The government sent a young man from Ottawa to raise a squadron of men from among the Mormons. This man was the kind of person who made enemies as soon as one met him. He had a little mustache, wore his hat on one side of his head, dressed like a fop, and in every way was disgusting to the hard-headed, rough-riding cowboy type of young men in the western provinces. This man spent one month in Cardston trying to get someone to join, but not even one man would sign up. Word quickly went back to Ottawa that the Mormons were disloyal and should be expelled from Canada.

We happened at that time to have a representative in the Canadian parliament, a Mr. W. A. Buchanan, from Lethbridge, Alberta, who was well acquainted with our people. He arose on the floor of the House and said, "If you will permit some of the young men of the Mormon church to go and qualify as officers, you will get all the men you want from that area, but they will not enlist under the kind of man you sent out."

The government told Mr. Buchanan that he would have the opportunity to test his faith and that he would be held responsible for the response. He thereafter got in touch with President Wood and told him to select four men to go to the camp in Calgary where they should qualify for officers. President Wood called me into his office and told me he was speaking with the advice of the First Presidency of the church and wanted me to go and qualify to become a senior officer among the Canadians. He also asked me to help him select four additional men besides me. The others included William Ainscough, Benjamin May, Andrew Woolf, and Hyrum Taylor.

Each of us went to the camp for several years, a few weeks at a time, from 1910 to 1912. I was first and qualified as a lieutenant, then as a captain, and later as a major. We took other men with us each year thereafter to the training camp in Calgary and established quite a reputation as we had a wonderful group. In 1914, however, war broke out between England and Germany, and, of course, this involved Canada.

Prior to the war, I had ridden as a cowboy for quite some time and had come across the Northwest Mounted Police—a fine force of well-trained men. They had outposts in various parts of the country. I was able to ride with them on some of their trips, to meet with them in their barracks, and I came to know them as a very outstanding group of men. I was, however, often challenged for my way of life, ridiculed because of my refusal to smoke and drink, and in other ways my faith was tested. All this is to say that I was not unacquainted with life in a military environment.

Still, when I first went up to the Calgary camp I had never stood at attention before and did not know what it was to line up. I was absolutely innocent of anything having to do with this side of the military. After the first day's exercises the captain who was in charge of the camp noted my awkwardness and called me into his office.

"I want to get a little better acquainted with you, Brown," he said. "Have a cigar."

"I don't smoke," I replied.

"Well, then, have a glass of beer."

"I don't drink, either."

Then he exclaimed, "The hell you don't!"

Some of the other officers who were present gave me the dickens when I came out of that interview.

"The captain was only trying to be sociable with you and you slapped him in the face," they said to me. "Haven't you got any sense?"

"If I have to do those things," I answered, "I don't want to be in the army at all." That put an end to that as far as I was concerned.

Another time at the Calgary camp, I remember a visiting colonel coming into my tent and asking, "I understand you have a good horse. May I ride him." I answered, of course, only later learning that the colonel was looking for the "best horse in Canada."

After his ride, the colonel asked me, "What will you take for him?"

"Five hundred dollars, " I replied immediately, thinking the price would be too high, since I had only paid $75 for the horse the previous year.

Without hesitating, the colonel said, "The horse is sold. I want you to deliver him next week."

Needless to say, this broke my heart, as I had become very much attached to this horse.

At the time I had bought the horse I had designated one of the men who I had been told was a horse trainer to take charge of him, to put him in good shape and have him ready for service in the summer. This he did in an expert manner, and I was very proud of my mount, Steamboat. I could ride him on the reservation, put the rein across his neck, and he would lie down. I could lie down beside him and fire my rifle and he would not move until I commanded. I could walk away from him, blow a whistle, and he would jump and come to my bidding. I learned to love him very much.

Two years later when I was in England I discovered the whereabouts of the colonel, now a general, to whom my horse had been sold and went over to his camp and found the horse in the stable. I went in and shouted his name. The horse jumped as though he had been shot. I put my arms around his neck and wept like a booby. I think the horse wept also. The general would not sell him, however, and I never saw him again.

When the war broke out in England I received a telegram from Ottawa asking me to raise a squadron to go overseas and giving me the rank of major in the overseas service. I became a member of an active military force. At the suggestion of David O. McKay, who had been called as an apostle of the church in 1906, I replied that I would do as requested. My wife, of course, was concerned and worried, but she never wavered one bit when she thought duty called me. We raised a squadron of men and became part of the 23rd Alberta Rangers. I gave my men their initial training in the army. That was one of the most enjoyable parts of my military career, training those young, raw recruits.

We trained from 1914 to 1916 in Canada. We were very proud of our outfit and especially of the men who could play musical instruments. We borrowed the instruments from the town, and my brother Lawrence was made leader of the band. They rehearsed and prepared themselves magnificently for their first appearance in Calgary, where they were given a great ovation. However, some months later, my commanding officer called me into his tent and told me he wanted me to turn the band and all the instruments over to another unit. I told him I could not, as the instruments belonged to the town of Cardston. He was very determined, and even though I returned the instruments to Cardston, he put a new man in charge of the band, very much to my regret and to the great disappointment of my brother, who thereupon returned to Cardston, not wishing to carry on after such treatment.

In June 1916, we went overseas. My wife, who was expecting a fourth child shortly, bade me goodbye at the railway station with her usual courage and fortitude. One month later, I received a cable saying she had given birth to another daughter. We had hoped for a son, but our daughter Mary came into our family, and I think her mother never did quite appreciate my comment when I replied to her notification of the birth by saying, "Don't have any more until I get home." This, I guess, was characteristic of my foolishness at the time.

In the meantime, we had changed the name of our regiment to the 13th Mounted Rifles. We enlisted as a group of cavalry men, but at that time it was discovered that the cavalry was no longer effective. It could no longer stand up against machine guns, so we were what they called "dismounted." Upon going overseas, however, we were broken up and became parts of other units whose numbers had been reduced by the war. This was discouraging since we had been bound together by the fact that we came from the same area and most of us were members of the same church.

One interesting incident in connection with our early days in the war took place in the fall of 1916, the year my daughter Mary was born. The Northwest Mounted Police, of whom I have already spoken, were very proud of their identity. One of the activities they enjoyed when not on duty was horseback wrestling. This consisted of two teams, ten in each team, facing each other at 100 yards distance without saddles. The teams would come at each other galloping and grapple. It was dangerous, but the Northwest Mounted Police could defeat any opponent they met up to that time because they had had a lot of practice at horseback wrestling.

The head of the police came to me one day and asked if I thought the Mormons would be willing to try themselves against the police in a public demonstration. I told him I was sure they would and added that I was sure they would win if they did. He, of course, thought this was ridiculous. But word went out that the Mormons and the police were going to meet in a horseback wrestling contest.

The time came for the contest. The police had said on many occasions they would teach those milk-fed Mormons how to wrestle. We happened to have in our squadron a number of professional wrestlers — not horseback wrestlers, but wrestlers who had developed their strength in their legs, arms, and shoulders. They were all good horsemen and could ride anything that wore hair. So when we met for the contest, more than 20,000 men had assembled to witness it. The two teams stood, and when the gun was fired they came together with a clash. When the clash was over, not one of the Mounted Police was left on his horse and not one Mormon had been dismounted. The leader of our group grabbed one policeman under each arm and took them to the end of the field. It was a startling thing to see and gave us a lot of fine publicity. I think it also made it easier from then on for us to be accepted by our associates in the army.

We had a man who was as tough as any man in the regiment. We called him the unsentimental cuss; he was the kind of man nobody liked. We thought he had no sense of emotion or of sympathy or of understanding, that he could see his comrades shot down by his side and never bat an eye. We did not think he had in him any sentiment at all. I was guilty of saying in my heart, "I thank thee, God, that I am not like that man." There was another Pharisee once who said that, and this time I was the Pharisee.

We were in France by this time. The unsentimental cuss was called on duty to examine the mail, incoming and outgoing mail, and he read a certain letter, a letter from a Mrs. Jock Anderson in London, Ontario, Canada. She was writing to her beloved Jock, and she said to him, "We are getting on all right, my dear. The ten little bairns are coming along. I have had to wean the baby because I have to work to support the others, but we are mighty proud of you and proud of where you are. But Jock, dear, our neighbor three months ago received word that her husband was missing. She said she had rather heard he was dead — she said she could hardly stand the uncertainty of it." And then she added, "Jock, my dear, join with me and pray God that I may never get word that you are missing."

The unsentimental officer read that letter but said nothing about it. That night there were paraded before him a sergeant and six men who were going out into no-man's land. They called the roll; the officer heard the name of Jock Anderson among those who were going out. The men went out, and in the morning the sergeant and three men came back. Again they called the roll, and Jock Anderson did not answer the roll call. The officer said to the sergeant, "Do you know where Jock Anderson fell?" The sergeant replied, "Yes, Sir, he fell on an elevation on which is trained the enemy's machine gun." The officer asked, "Do you think a man could go out to that body and get the identification disk off his neck?" The sergeant answered, "Sir, it would be absolute suicide, but if you say so I will try." Then the officer said, "I didn't mean that. I just wanted to know."

In the first world war a man could not be declared dead unless his body or his identification disk could be produced. That night the unsentimental officer was missing, and the next morning there came up to the front lines a large regimental envelope. When it was opened an identification disk fell out with the name of Jock Anderson on it and a short note which read, "Dear Major: I am enclosing the identification disk of Jock Anderson. Please write to Mrs. Anderson in London, Ontario, Canada, and tell her God heard her prayer — her husband is not missing."

That was the man of whom I had said, "I thank thee, God, that I am not like him." He had the courage which I never had to crawl out on his stomach in the face of almost certain death in order to bring to a woman he had never seen the poor comfort that her husband was not missing. On the bottom of his letter he wrote, as though it did not amount to much, "As for me, I am off for blighty in the morning. The doctor says it is an amputation case and may prove fatal. Cheerio." Since that experience I have tried to believe that every man has something in him worth saving.

On several occasions in England and France, appeals came to me from some of the boys who were sick in the hospital, asking me to intercede for them with officers higher up, asking that they might be returned home while they were convalescing; asking, perhaps, that they might have leave of absence.

In London, one morning, I received a message that some boy wanted to see me in the hospital; and immediately I thought, here is another boy who would like to return to his mother, who perhaps will ask me to intercede for him. As I went to the hospital, I felt just a little pride in my heart because I had the honor of wearing an officer's uniform. By virtue of that fact I held the right to intercede as an officer of the king.

With this feeling I went into the hospital, and as I was ushered into the little ward where that boy was sick, he reached out to me with a feeble hand and said, "Brother Brown, I sent for you to come and administer to me; I'm afraid I'm going to die, and I want you to ask God to spare my life that I can return home to my mother."

It seemed to me that my uniform fell from me. All the pride that I had felt in standing in that uniform vanished. At that moment I was made to realize that there is an authority, there is a power inestimably greater than any authority or power that can be given by man. As I laid my hands upon the head of that boy, I interceded for him, not with the King of England, not by virtue of my authority as an officer in that army, but in the name of Jesus Christ and by the authority of the holy priesthood. And as I knelt there, my prayer to God was that never again in my life would I be found seeking the honors of men. I went into that hospital a proud British officer; I came out a humble Mormon Elder.

We stayed in England from 1916 and part of 1917, training and transporting men across the channel. I made a number of trips into France from England at the head of troops which were taken up by local units in groups of ten, twenty, thirty, or fifty men. After each trip I would return to England for more troops. That was my job.

While at Shorncliff, during the spring of 1917, I believe, I had the opportunity of meeting the commander of all the Canadian forces in Europe, General Turner. All my military life I had looked forward to the time when I could become a high-ranking officer, and it appeared as though that time was coming because at Shorncliff, where we were stationed, there was just one man between me and that position. This man soon became a casualty of the war, and I received a wire from General Turner to come to

London. I was sure I was going to be nominated as the next in command of the Shorncliff area.

Upon arriving, however, I found the general had already made up his mind that I was not to be appointed. He rather apologetically, although bluntly, told me that he could not make the appointment. "You have all the qualifications necessary, you have passed all the examinations, you have had the experience of leading men," he said, "but I cannot make the appointment."

He then went into an adjoining office to answer a telephone, and, in his absence, I looked on his desk and saw my military record sheet. Across the bottom of it was written in block capitals THIS MAN IS A MORMON. I knew then why he could not make the assignment, but that did not make the disappointment any less difficult for me. When he returned, he said, "That's all, Brown," and I left.

This was one of the most disappointing and difficult experiences of my life, and, as far as I know, the only rebuff I ever encountered on account of my religion.

When I arrived back at Shorncliff that day, I challenged the Lord for having denied me what I thought was my right. I asked him, "How could you do this to me? When I have been true and faithful all the way through my military career, why do you now cut me down?" I was young, ambitious, vigorous, and would have accepted the post had it been offered to me. Then I heard the voice, my voice, talking to the currant bush back home three years earlier. The voice said to me, "I am the gardener here, and I know what I want you to be." I had completely forgotten my experience with the currant bush and recognized immediately that my voice to the currant bush had become God's voice to me. It continued, "Someday, when you are laden with fruit, you will thank me for cutting you down, for not submitting to your wish and not appointing you to what you wanted to have."

I now realize, more than fifty years later, that God is truly the gardener. He knows what he wants each of us to be. I have not amounted to very much in this life as it is, but I believe I have done better than I would have done if the Lord had let me go the way I wanted to go.

Soon after this experience, I was informed by the commanding officer that my services would not be required further in that connection, that I was to return to Canada to become a transport officer and to train new troops.

This further greatly disappointed me as I had been instrumental in enlisting all the men who were serving under me. Many of them had come because I was at the head. Their parents knew me and had faith in me since I had been a member of a bishopric and was active in the church. I knew they would look upon me as something of a quitter since a number of their sons had been killed in action and I seemed to be turning my back on them and was going home. I told the commanding officer that I would be willing to revert to a lower rank, provided he would let me go on to France. But he said, "No, you are needed in Canada as a training and transport officer."

I returned to Canada and, as anticipated, received a very cold reception. Many of the parents of boys who had been lost in the war refused to shake hands with me. I was looked down upon by them. Some of them misunderstood what was going on and they treated me with considerable contempt. This was very hard to take and was one of the most trying experiences of my life — one in which my wife participated loyally, but also with a heartbroken spirit because so many of our friends had turned their backs on us and called me a coward and a quitter. That May I recorded the following in my journal:

> I spent most of the month of May at home visiting family and friends and learned by bitter experience of being misjudged, for some who had appeared to be my friends were most harsh in their criticism of my returning home, thinking I came on account of my fear of the battle line. But God knows I did not have any choosing and that I tried to do my duty and play the game.

Later on, in the spring of 1918, I left with another draft of fifteen hundred men for England and France. Enroute we stopped at Pettawawa, Ontario, which was a large camp where the men were held pending the availability of transportation as the submarine activity was very sharp at the time. When we stopped in

Pettawawa, I took my fifteen hundred men into the camp. There were about 4,500 men already in the camp, so my group made it 6,000 men in all.

No one could leave the camp because a ship could become available at any time. Consequently the men became restless. Many were convicts who had been taken out of jail and put into the military. Some of the men in my group had to be chained to their seats while we crossed the country because they had escaped many times previously. Needless to say, I had a very hard time with some of them.

One morning, at around 2 a.m., the sergeant major, who was a veteran of the Boer War in South Africa and a very good soldier, came to my tent and said, "Sir, the men are all rioting. They are tearing down their tents and destroying the furnishings. It is a serious situation. I suggest you let me go up there with all the officers I can muster, with our pistols, our side arms, and try to put down the riot." I told him immediately that we would not go up there armed in any respect. We would all go up as he had recommended but we would leave our pistols in our tents.

When we arrived at the main place where the men had all assembled and were tearing down their tents, I got up on one of the tables and started to talk. In the language of the profession, these men were "raising hell." This was when I first fully realized the value of street preaching. Shortly after beginning to speak, I was hit in the back of the head by a tent peg. This slowed me down for some time but I recovered and went on talking. I talked from 2 a.m. until 5 a.m. and finally got the ear of these men. They eventually went back quietly and put up their tents. I told them they could sleep in the next morning and there would be no action taken against them. The next morning I had seventy-five of them parade in my tent for discipline. Among these were the ten ringleaders. I gave the others a stern rebuke but took these ten men into custody. I think in all of my experiences I never made a talk quite as convincing as the talk I made under those very trying and severe circumstances.

We continued on for a few days and then went overseas. My draft of 1,500 men was broken up among the various units, thereby relieving me of my command. In the fall of 1918 the war was over and we were all able to return home to our wives and families.

CHAPTER 4

LAW AND FAMILY LIFE

A ll my life I had hoped someday to become a lawyer, although it frankly looked impossible to me because I did not have the formal training. I did not have credits enough to be admitted to the Law Society of Alberta, which was a prerequisite to enrolling as a student of law in the office of a barrister of law, where one could study the law while also practicing it.

Around 1914 I wrote to the president of the University of Alberta and told him of my experiences, including my mission in England, and thought that he might be able to make an exception in my case and permit me to join the Law Society and become a student of law. He replied that I would need at least two more years of formal training in order to qualify. This news was very discouraging to me because Zina and I were barely getting by and could not afford to leave income-producing work to go away to school. I was quite downcast.

Just then there was a conference of the Alberta Stake meeting in Cardston and the president of the university happened to be in Cardston enroute to the Waterton Lakes. He came to the meeting and was invited to sit on the stand with the rest of the leaders. At the opening of the meeting, Elder David O. McKay, who was the presiding church authority, said, "We are going to ask Elder Hugh B. Brown to be the speaker today as we have a number of distinguished visitors. Brother Brown has recently been on a mission and can represent the church."

Well, I spoke on the first principles of the gospel and the Restoration. As I sat down I sat next to this man who was the president of the university.

"Are you the Mr. Brown who wrote to me about joining the Law Society?" he turned to me and asked.

"Yes, sir," I answered.

"I turned you down, didn't I?"

"Yes, you did."

"If you will write me tomorrow morning, I'll change the verdict. No one can talk like you talked today and not be entirely entitled to become a law student."

This has to be the most profitable sermon I ever preached. It cut out two years of preparation, and I became what people would call a "fluke." I was admitted to the Law Society and almost immediately signed up with B. H. Elton of Lethbridge.

After getting on with Mr. Elton, the war in Europe broke out and he told me that he thought the Law Society would give me credit for the time I was in the service provided I would do certain reading during that time. I was a voracious reader and undertook to read everything I could get. Mr. Elton gave me some regular textbooks, which I read very carefully while I was in the army.

In 1918, after returning home, I took up residence in Cardston and transferred my apprenticeship to the office of Zebulon W. Jacobs, a lawyer who was practicing in Cardston. Mr. Jacobs paid me $35 a month, and I did all the work in his office, such as scrubbing the floor, making the fires every morning, polishing the stove, and, as it turned out, delivering much of his mail by hand to save on stamps. I worked in Mr. Jacobs's office from 1918 to 1921, during which time I only got $35 a month and had a family at that time of five children. Besides Zina and Zola, we had also had June, born on 27 June 1914, Mary, born on 8 August 1916, and Hugh, born on 22 October 1919.

Upon the birth of my first son, I wrote in my journal, "He is a joy to the household and the cause of continuing thanksgiving to his parents. May we have wisdom to care for, train, and direct the footsteps of these precious jewels so that our old age may be made glorious by the knowledge of their worthy achievements and faithfulness to the truth."

As a legal apprentice, I was expected to do all the necessary leg work. I prepared claims or answers to claims. I took estates and prepared everything in connection with them. I prepared wills and had them executed in the proper way. So that when I got through with my apprenticeship, I knew most of the procedures of the court and the office and was able to take over the practice of law on my own when I was finally admitted. This was a real advantage, as I learned afterwards, that many young men who came directly from law schools did not have. As a matter of fact, I once asked one very brilliant young man in our office to prepare an estate for probate. He replied, "What do I do first?" He did not know how to start or to proceed. I had to help him as a novice practically. Unfortunately, the man for whom I worked took no interest in us except to answer questions that came up in the course of our regular studies. It was a hard way to learn the law, but it was very thorough.

I knew that the final examinations were going to be difficult since I had been separated from that kind of reading during my absence in Europe. At that time, however, I met a young man named Chauncey E. Snow, who was also expecting to write off his final examinations, and we did some studying together. He was a brilliant young student but was going through the same process that I had undertaken. However, he had more formal schooling than I and was better trained in the matter of how to study. So I welcomed his assistance in reading and discussing problems having to do with those phases of the law which I thought would become subject for discussion in the final examinations.

While working as Zeb Jacobs's law clerk, I decided to provide better accommodations for my family. To that end I purchased what was known in Cardston at the time as the Cazier Place for $4,600. This was one of the largest homes in the city and was somewhat glamorous in that it had stylish architecture, a good location, and a history. I purchased it before selling my other home and made arrangements to pay for it on a partial payment system. While living there, during 1919 and the early part of 1920, I finished my final studies in law.

During this time I also purchased what was known as the Anderson farm, about two miles south of Cardston, for $7,500. I had the idea that I could make some money on milk, eggs, cream, butter, as well as other farm produce. We were fairly successful at that. I found that it was necessary for me to get up early in the morning to read. Often I would be at my job by 3 a.m., where I would study until 6:00 or 6:30, then do the chores on the farm and be in the office at 9:00 in Cardston.

At the university we were given an outline to study of various subjects such as torts, contracts, international law, etc., and were told of certain books we should read, which we did. In the main I purchased the books on those topics and developed somewhat of a law library. This was very helpful as I could take it around with me while traveling on my church work, for I was at the time a member of the high council of the Lethbridge Stake, which necessitated my weekend traveling to the outlying wards.

I felt the need of reading up on history especially, and there came into town agents from book companies whom I contacted. I arranged to sell certain books for them in return for which I would obtain other books which they were offering. For instance, I sold four sets of what was called "The Five-Foot Shelf," or *Harvard Classics*, and then received my own set of fifty volumes. I read assiduously from these volumes as they covered most of the areas in which I was interested. In fact, this was a set of books from which one could get information on almost any subject.

I became acquainted with the works of Will Durrant, a philosopher. I also read carefully the works of Albert J. Beveridge. His *Life of John Marshall* gave me the determination I needed to follow through on my legal studies. Many times I had wondered if I was doing the right thing. My family was deprived of some of the things they might have otherwise had, although I must say that in the main they never wanted for anything. I had been successful in getting enough real estate work and insurance business to supplement my meager legal salary. We survived on that. Also, I took over the management of the Cahoon Hotel and moved my family into that for a time, which was a good thing for us. It provided light, heat, shelter, and a good income. I could lock myself off in a room and study early, late, and sometimes in mid-day.

Besides these books, I also acquired the great poets. I became familiar with William Shakespeare and Thomas Carlyle. I liked Ralph Waldo Emerson's, William Wordsworth's, and Sir Walter

Scot's works. I gradually built up a substantial library—one at which I worked all the time.

My wife often said that during these years she was only acquainted with that part of my face she could see above a book or a newspaper. I am afraid I was not a very good husband or father at that time. Getting up at 3 a.m., studying for a few hours, then doing the chores, going to the law office, doing a little real estate work, coming home, doing the chores again, and reading again at night—not much of my time, if any, was given to my children. They were, of course, in school, and my wife was a great support to me through it all. She believed in me when I, at times, lost faith in myself. She would say, "You must stay with it, we must see it through together. It will be a great boon in our lives to have you become a lawyer, for this will introduce you to many things you otherwise would not get." This proved to be prophetic as many times since being admitted to the bar I have had things come my way because I was known as a lawyer which I would not have had otherwise.

I worked for Zeb Jacobs until late 1920 or early 1921 when I decided to move my family to Lethbridge. I knew that if I was successful in passing the law examinations I would have to have a larger range of clients than was possible in Cardston. I purchased a good home in Lethbridge, one that was quite beyond what we could afford, but good fortune was with me. I had first found a quarter section of land east of Lethbridge that was for sale at twenty dollars an acre. I did not have any money, but I arranged to pay the down payment by borrowing from a friend. Then I found the home I wanted.

It was a new home. The man who built it was a builder himself and was living in it at the time, but his health had failed and he was leaving for California. He had put his house on the market for $15,000 which was a big price for a home. I told him I would take it if he would take this quarter section of land. He asked what the area was worth, and I said forty dollars an acre. He readily approved. A quarter section is 160 acres, so this made a rather substantial down payment. Of course, I had to pay out the balance I owed on the section at twenty dollars an acre, but this gave me a profit of twenty dollars an acre. We sold the Cazier

Place in Cardston and moved to Lethbridge. I began the appren-ticeship to David H. Hilton, and Chauncey Snow came to live with us in the home. He and I worked together on our legal stud-ies, which was fortunate for me since by discussing issues with him I could impress upon my own mind the facts I would oth-erwise have overlooked.

On 20 July 1921 Chauncy and I went up to Calgary where we passed the final examination of the Law Society and received our certificates as full-fledged barristers and solicitors in the prov-ince of Alberta. I wrote in my journal,

> I am at last a barrister with authority to practice in the Supreme Court of Alberta. We had some little difficulties during the time I was a student but were blessed of the Lord and are better off finan-cially than when we started to study. My wife has been a very faith-ful support and help in all of the course, and I hope to make good in this profession.

I immediately opened a little office of my own in downtown Lethbridge, took what few books I had, brought a chair, a table, and a desk, and hoped for some clients. Within a matter of weeks Mr. Hjalmar Ostlund, who was practicing law across the street from where my little office stood, was suddenly taken ill. His doctors recommended that he leave and go to California for at least three months. He asked if I would come and take charge of his office during his absence. In return, I could share his fees. That is, I would try the cases he had ready for trial and take care of his current business, and he would pay me a proportion of the amount that was received in fees on the work I did. This was a real break for me as he had a large clientele and a lot of cases to try.

This occurred in the fall of that year. He had a lot on the docket, and I tried all the cases that came in. He stayed away six months instead of three, and when he got home I had cleaned up all the cases on the docket. I had become acquainted with a lot of his clients and had his office in good shape. When he came home he was so well pleased with what I had done that he offered me a partnership on a 60/40 percent basis. This was satisfactory for the first year, at the end of which he gave me a 50/50 contract. This turned out very well. I made better than $10,000. The third year we renegotiated our arrangement and I was given 60 percent of all fees, while he received 40 percent. This lasted from 1921 to 1927.

I had one case during these years that I will never forget. A woman from what is known today as the Crow's Nest Pass — the towns west of Cardston and up in the Canadian Rockies — had killed a man who had attempted to assault her. She came to my office when I was there alone.

"I want to retain your services," she said. "I killed this man, and I want you to know that I expect to pay for it with my life. But I am told I will have to employ a lawyer, so will you come?"

At the time, we were attorneys for the labor union of which her husband was a member, and we told her we would take the case. I went up to her home in the Crow's Nest and got all the details of the murder. But she repeated again and again that she intended to pay for her murder by sacrificing her own life. I told her that she was not guilty of murder in the strict sense, that it was a matter of self defense and therefore not murder. I had a hard time convincing her of that, but I thought I had finally convinced her.

The case was to be tried before the trial division of the Supreme Court of Alberta, and it was several months before the court would next sit in that area. This was also the first case that I had tried before the supreme court since becoming a partner with Hjalmar Ostlund. When the court opened on the morning of the trial and this woman was arraigned, the clerk read the charge and then asked, "Are you guilty or not?"

She paused for a moment and then turned to the judge and said, "I am guilty, my lord, I don't care what my lawyer says."

Whereupon the judge turned to me and asked, "What are you going to do with that, Mr. Brown?"

I replied, "I am pleading for her, as she does not understand the law, and I am pleading not guilty."

We went ahead and tried the case, and, of course, she was exonerated. The next morning the papers came out with the headline: "Woman Says She is Guilty, Court Says She Lies."

The sequel to that is that this woman had not paid us anything up to that time. As I had spent so much time on the case, her bill amounted to quite a little money. A few days after the trial, we received word that she had hanged herself in her orchard near her home. And we never did receive anything for what we had done.

Another case which attracted considerable attention in the area was that of a man in North Dakota who had bought quite a large farm in Alberta and who had sent his nephew up from North Dakota to handle the farm on a share basis. The man stayed several years on the farm, and they both seemed to get along well. Eventually, however, the uncle decided that his nephew was getting too much and refused to compensate him, whereupon we started suit against him.

This was one of the cases where it was necessary to have what is called "an examination for discovery." I went down to North Dakota and employed a court reporter for the uncle's deposition. During the trial, the uncle contradicted his earlier statements, and I would say, "In North Dakota you said thus and so, but now you are saying the opposite. When are you lying, then or now?"

This man was a doctor by profession and a fine looking man, and it grieved him greatly to be called a liar in public. I tried to be as merciful as I could, but that was the crux of my examination, to prove that he had admitted certain things in the original examination which he now denied. He became so excited that he fainted and fell out of the witness box, which on that occasion was elevated above where the judge sat, and in Canada all witnesses stand throughout the examination, as do the attorneys. I caught him as he fell and carried him out of the court room into the chambers of the judge.

The man on the other side of the case, a Mr. Jameson, was a very prominent lawyer in Lethbridge and Calgary. It took us several days to try the case. Witnesses were brought in from North Dakota and a number from Alberta. I was particularly pleased to win the case because, as it turned out, it was taken to the supreme court of Alberta on appeal, giving me a chance to make some additional pleas and to try out my ability in preparing briefs for the appeal.

The appeal court sat in Calgary, so we went from Lethbridge to Calgary to try the appeal. Mr. Jameson presented his case in a very able manner. After he had proceeded, I began to lose some confidence in my own brief. I saw some holes that I had left open, but just as he sat down, suddenly a thought came to me that I might win the good will of the court by explaining to them that I had so much confidence in their perception that it would not be necessary for me to present my case, since everything I had to say was in the brief and it would waste the time of the court to go through it. The chief justice said, "Thank you very much, Mr. Brown. We appreciate your thoughtfulness and consideration. The appeal is dismissed." I was very grateful for their decision, since this was the first time I stood in the presence of five solemn looking, robed justices, and I was very timid.

I practiced law from 1921 to 1927 with Hjalmar Ostlund and P. Drew Clark, who, as a new lawyer, had come into our office on a small consideration. We developed quite a big practice, had many cases to try, and I did much more legal practice there than I did later in Salt Lake City, although I was a member of the bar in Salt Lake City for a much longer time.

During those six years in Canada, I was exposed to all kinds of law: criminal, civil, and petty cases. I was partly responsible for the small debts law which provided that plaintiffs could cite their own cases and be heard without having to go through the necessary red tape of a regular action for cases involving small amounts. Anything under two hundred dollars was to be tried in this small courts claim department, saving time for both lawyers and clients. I say that I was partially responsible because I defended the proposed law to the court on a special hearing, after which it was submitted to the legislature, where it passed and became the law of Alberta.

On 24 October 1923, I turned forty years old. The following day I wrote in my journal,

> I have passed another milestone in life. Yesterday, the 24th, was my birthday, being my 40th. I had thought that I would have made more of a mark in life than I have done and no doubt could have done if I had taken advantage of all my opportunities. I find now that my plans, hopes, and aspirations are centered in my family. The Lord has blessed me with a most devoted and capable wife. In all of my travels I have never seen one who could so fill the place of

wife and mother. Our six children are well and happy and we feel greatly blessed in them. I give considerable time to the church and public work but I am more than compensated in the joy that comes from service.

Four months after I was admitted to the bar in 1921, when I was thirty-seven, the church authorities decided to organize a new stake in the area—the Lethbridge Stake—made up of wards formerly belonging to the Alberta and Taylor stakes. The new stake was organized by Rudger Clawson and John Wells, and I was installed as president of the stake. This was a rather heavy assignment in view of the fact that I had just been admitted to the bar and was trying to get started. In addition, the stake was widely scattered. It extended from the international boundary north to the North Pole, as far as I knew, and along the east boundary of the province of Alberta, encompassing all of Alberta that was not included in the other two stakes.

Sometimes in traveling throughout the stake we would journey as many as 1,800 miles to go from our headquarters out to the wards and back. Often the weather was such that we were out almost all night and frequently in inclement weather. The temperature sometimes registered forty-five degrees below zero. The cars were, according to present standards, inadequate, and roads were almost non-existent. We often had to get out and kick the mud out from between the wheels and the fenders. My counselors at the time were George W. Green and Asael E. Palmer. Brother Green was head of the Ellison Milling Company in Alberta and Brother Palmer was with the Experimental Station, a federal institution located in Lethbridge. They were both capable and wonderful men.

We organized the stake, set up the wards, appointed new bishops, and generally went about setting things in order. We made what I think was a churchwide record our second year. We were organized in 1921 and at the beginning of 1922 determined that every member living within the stake would pay a full tithing. We concentrated on that for the whole year, and at the end of the year we achieved our goal. There was not a man, woman, or child in the stake who had a dollar who had not tithed it. I think the brethren in Salt Lake City did not fully appreciate what we did on that occasion, but I doubt that it has ever been equalled any-where since.

We had a glorious time. We had a wonderful stake organiza-tion and a lot of good wards. I tried to put into practice what Bishop Harris had taught me so many years earlier about toler-ance, understanding, and seeing beyond the smoke of a cigarette and into the soul of a man. To illustrate this, I would like to cite the following experience.

We had for sometime been looking for a bishop for the Tabor Ward—Tabor being a ward about forty miles southeast of Lethbridge—but we could not find the right man on the records. We were acquainted with practically all of them, so the three of us—my two counselors and I—got in my car and started for Tabor. As we were driving along we beheld a car approaching us in the opposite direction. I immediately recognized the driver and hailed him to stop. He stopped and got out of the car. He was smoking a cigar.

After exchanging pleasant greetings and talking for a time, I said, "Burt, we want you to be the bishop of the Tabor Ward."

He held up his cigar and asked, "Hell, with this?"

I answered, "Hell, no. Without it."

He threw it down on the ground, stepped on it, and said, "By hell, I'll try it."

He never smoked again and became one of the best bishops we had. In fact, he did away with cigarette smoking entirely in his ward. This was an incident in which we were not bound by the strict rules of the law but could forgive and utilize the abili-ties of men despite some obvious weaknesses.

While we were living in Lethbridge in the new house we had purchased, most of our children were in school. Zina turned twelve years old during this time, and the rest ranged down to Charles Manley, who was born on 19 November 1921, and to Margaret, born on 9 January 1927. The family's health was pretty good. We had the usual colds and childhood diseases, such as chicken pox, mumps, measles, and so forth. But all in all we enjoyed good health. The children all participated with their mother in doing the housework, and we lived a happy life. I give to my wife the credit for the spirit of our home and for the love that predominated. Never once during my life with Zina, which now exceeds sixty years, did I ever hear her raise her voice in the home to any of our children. Yet she always had complete obedience from them and exerted a tremendous effect upon my own life as I observed her charity, her love, her kindness, and her devotion.

My duties as a lawyer and as president of the stake took practically all of my time. The raising of the family was pretty much in the hands of their mother. Perhaps this was fortunate for the family. I think I gave them all the time I could and did the things I had to do in the law and in the church, but of course I think I could have done better by them if I had given them more time. Fortunately, Zina was of a nature to take on the additional load, without complaint, and very efficiently.

One event occurred while I was stake president that is worth noting. At one of our stake conferences in Lethbridge, where I was presiding and where I spoke, there was in attendance, without my knowledge, a woman from eastern Canada. She was very intelligent and literary. She came up to me at the close of conference and asked, "Are you available, sir, to transfer to some other part of the country?"

"Under what circumstances?" I replied.

"We'll pay up to $12,500 to get the man we want as our minister is leaving us. I can recommend you to the rest of the congregation for that amount, and perhaps it could be arranged for more, if you desire."

I explained to her my situation. I could not take her offer.

She then asked, "Does you church pay you more than that?"

"Well, hardly," I said, "but I cannot take your offer."

It was a direct offer of $12,500 or, as she intimated, $15,000 a year, including a house to live in and all expenses paid. It was frankly a pretty nice offer, but not one a Latter-day Saint could accept.

Another event occurred in one of our meetings of the stake presidency and high council—one which I think no one who was present will ever forget. We had made our reports, had borne our testimonies, and were about to dismiss, when suddenly I said to them, "Brethren, I have an impression that I know what each of you will come to."

Then, starting with the senior member, I went around the circle and told each one his weaknesses, his shortcomings, his failings, as well as his strengths, his aptitudes, and his abilities, and pleaded with them to measure up to their potential. I think I have never been more inspired in any effort, and never has a group responded more wholeheartedly than they did. Many of them confided to me afterwards that I told them things that no one else knew. Drew Clark was clerk at the time and he made a record of that meeting, although this did not become a part of the public record.

By 1925 our income was better than $20,000 a year from my practice. We had little reason for leaving Lethbridge, except for the fact that there were very few Latter-day Saints there. I had four young daughters and two sons, and I felt that they were entitled to associations other than those they were getting. In talking this over with my wife, we decided that whatever the sacrifice we would move to Salt Lake City, or to that region, where we could enjoy more LDS associations. None of the officials in the city of Lethbridge or in the schools were members of our church, and our young people were sometimes snubbed and even mistreated in the schools because of their religious convictions. This was the motivating factor that caused us to leave Canada.

I wrote directly to President Heber J. Grant and told him of our situation, of our feelings that we would like to move and get established while our children were still young enough to have meaningful associations with other LDS people. He wrote back immediately and said, "You are at liberty to move any time you desire. We understand the situation and will reorganize the stake as soon as you advise us of the time of your leaving." The brethren were very gracious, which we greatly appreciated.

When we finally decided to move to Salt Lake City in 1926, with the approval of the brethren, the stake was reorganized and my second counselor, Asael Palmer, was made stake president. The members in Lethbridge gave us a good, warm send off. I left my family there to come down to make arrangements first for a place to live. At the time, we thought we were going to Logan, as a lawyer was just leaving Logan and wanted to sell his practice. I thought I could purchase his practice and establish a good law firm there. But immediately after arriving in Salt Lake City I was stricken with the tic douloureux, a severe attack of nerves starting from the large nerve leading off the base of the brain which speads over the side of the head and results in excruciating pain. It occurred intermittently over the next twenty or so years, but while it was on it was almost unbearable.

I say I was stricken right after I came to Salt Lake City, but in fact I had had some trouble before leaving Lethbridge. At first, I went to several dentists thinking it had something to do with my teeth. They agreed with my diagnosis and pulled some of my teeth but found nothing wrong. Finally, one of them said, "You should go to a regular physician." I did, and he said to me, "God have mercy on your soul. You have what is known as the worst, most painful, most discouraging affliction known. You should go down to Salt Lake City immediately where they have special facilities for caring for this kind of trouble." He then injected my nerve with alcohol. This became necessary to do from time to time to assuage the pain and to enable me to carry on.

While waiting in Salt Lake City with the tic douloureux, I met Albert E. Bowen. He asked me where I was going to practice law and I told him Logan.

"You are foolish," he said, "I practiced there for some years and finally came to Salt Lake. If you go to Logan now it will just mean that you will have to move twice, because you will come here in a few years anyway."

He persuaded me that stopping off in Logan was not the right thing to do. I had, in the meantime, virtually closed a deal with Mariner Eccles on a large home he had on Center Street in Logan, but we had not closed the deal, and when I changed my mind to come to Salt Lake City instead, I purchased a home at 1354 Stratford Avenue. This was a very fine home that had been built by Claude Richards but which was in the hands of a bank. I purchased it for $14,000, but with very little down, as I had not sold my home in Lethbridge.

I knew that this was the home for us even before I went into it. Stayner Richards was the real estate agent, and as we came around the corner on 1300 East and I saw it in the distance, I said out loud, "That's the home I want." He quoted me the price. I went to the bank to arrange for the terms and purchased the home. When my family came down they were all delighted with it as it was the best home we had had up to that time. We lived there from 1927 to 1937.

CHAPTER 5

SALT LAKE CITY

A s I indicated, my purpose in leaving Canada and returning to the United States was to give my children the advantage of better associations than they had had in Lethbridge.
I came to Salt Lake City in early 1927 and entered into the
Eddington–Cope Radio Company as a manager. I fooled around
with this for a year without any success and then became a partner in 1928 with Robert Murray Stewart, a son-in-law of future
church president George Albert Smith, in his law practice. We
were together a little over a year when I received an attractive
offer from the law firm of J. Reuben Clark, Preston D. Richards,
and Albert E. Bowen for a similar partnership arrangement, which
I took.

I came into their firm on the understanding that we should
all share on an equal basis, and for some years this relationship
was quite successful. One of my clients, the Deseret Mortuary
Company, was paying me a retainer of $10,000 a year, and this
helped considerably. Our new house on Stratford Avenue in Salt
Lake City was the nicest house we ever owned. All the family
look back on it as their family home. My law practice increased
steadily. My income was fairly good, and we were very happy.

At this time, and because of the Deseret Mortuary Company,
my practice had more to do with corporate law than with anything else. This necessitated that I travel to all of the western states.
They had established mortuaries in Utah, Idaho, Montana, Washington, Oregon, Nevada, and, I think, Arizona.

It was during these trips, and especially because of my letters
home to my family, that I realized that we cannot always express
all we think and that we feel some things which are deeper than
thought. Each one of us lives in a world of his own. His friends

and even his nearest relatives only see the margin of his life with an occasional glimpse of the "inland."

I have often wished I had the power to portray to my audiences what I feel—that the best of both thought and feeling would not be lost on the threshing floor of speech. Only now and then do we get a golden kernel. Most of the best is too subtle to be caught in the mortal burlap which we hang over the spout.

Two of the letters I wrote to my family, the first to my son Hugh and the second to my wife, Zina, during one of these many, often lonely, trips follow:

Portland, Oregon
October 19th, 1930

My Dear Son;-

It is Sunday and I am alone in the hotel. I am to leave for Washington tomorrow so will not have a chance to write you before your birthday. I left a little present with you before I left home but want to write you so you will get it on your birthday as my love for you is more than any little present which I might give you.

You are rapidly growing into a man. It will not be long before you will be earning your own way in the world and learning many of the things which every man must learn. Your success or failure will depend more on yourself than on where you are or what you have or do not have. If a fellow will always do only the things which he knows he should do, if he will always refuse to do anything which he would not like to have his friends know about, in other words if he will shoot straight and play fair he will make a success of his life.

Too many men and boys seem to think success is a matter of the money they have or the position they hold. Place and position and money do not make a man good or bad. Whether he is good or bad, a success or a failure depends on himself, on what he thinks of himself and on how genuine he is.

I had two horses and I want to tell you about them. One was a fine bay mare. She had a glossy coat, held her head high and looked like a thoroughbred. Everyone loved to look at her and would say, "Isn't she a beauty, I'd like to own her." She was like some rich men, she had a fine appearance and attracted attention but she was not reliable. When I would ride her she would rear over backwards or try to buck me off. When I would drive her she would run away at the first opportunity and if I had her on a loaded wagon she would quit me whenever I got in a mud hole or on a hill. Just when I wanted to depend on her she would fail me. In other words she could not be depended upon. Her name was Bell and although she came from good stock she just did not have it in her to be a good reliable horse.

The other horse was named Dan. He was a grey gelding, not nearly as pretty to look at as Bell. He did not hold his head as high and did not attract the attention of the people who came to the ranch. He did not show off at all and most men who would judge horses by their outward appearance would have chosen Bell instead of Dan if they had been buying a horse. However, when I wanted a good horse to ride, one that would take me to the end of the road, or when I had a big load to haul over a bad road where real honest work was necessary, when I wanted to depend on real service I always took Dan instead of Bell. Men and horses are a lot alike. Some are all for show and make believe but cannot be depended on to do a real job.

It is more important what we think of ourselves than what others think of us. We ourselves know whether we are honest, whether we are what we want others to think we are or whether we are just bluffing. And what we are is more important than what people think we are. Sometime people will find out just what we are and that is when we will be glad we have been fair and not tried to make believe. No one likes a baulky horse or a dishonest man.

Whenever a man or boy does anything in secret that he would not have others know of he is dishonest and whenever he yields to temptation to do wrong he is weakening himself and losing strength which he will need later in life. Each man and boy is given charge of his own life to make a success or a failure and what he has or where he is going does not matter much. Integrity is what counts. Integrity is what a horse has when he carries you to the end of the road or pulls you out of a mud hole or does not kick or strike you. Integrity is what my good horse Dan had when I was riding him on the Indian Reserve and got lost in a blizzard. I did not know which way to go home. I knew it was about thirty miles away but I did not know which way to go. If I did not get home that night I was sure I should freeze on the prairie. I took old Dan's bridle off and sat in the saddle for several hours not knowing where he was taking me but sure he would be honest with me. Finally he stopped. It was snowing so hard that I could not see three feet ahead of me so I got off to see why he had stopped and there was the gate to our own field. He had taken me home and saved my life. If I had been riding Bell she would likely have bucked me off in a snow bank and run off and left me to die. Oh it is fine to be dependable, honest, and trustworthy.

Now, my son, it is not my purpose to write you a long letter of instruction, but your Daddy is expecting you to be a great and good man and he knows that much depends on what kind of a boy you are. A good colt usually grows into a good horse and a bad colt into a bad horse. So good boys make good men and bad boys bad men. Just tell yourself that you are going to be a fine man and then think of that every time you are tempted to do anything you should not do and you will be suprised what you can make yourself do. People will love you for what you are and not for what you own. You may have lived eleven years. When you have lived another eleven you will be a man and your character will be formed. The next eleven years are very important in your life so watch them carefully and make every one of them count for good.

There is another thing you must remember and that is that those of your brothers and sisters who are younger than you will follow your example and will do what they see you do so you must be very careful what kind of example you set them. I have five brothers younger than I and four sisters, and I always felt that I must not lead them away from the right path in life. So I refused to smoke or drink or swear or steal or lie because I did not want them to do those things, as if they learned them from me I should be responsible.

You have a fine mind. The Lord has given you much natural ability and He expects much from you. He wants you for His servant so prepare yourself for His service. Keep your body clean top. Then I saw that I was carrying in my hand some kind of vessel, which I dropped. It fell down the well of the winding stairs and crashed at the bottom. I had to return to the bottom and pass many of my friends who were climbing up. But as I started to climb up the stairs again, I passed many of these same friends and eventually mangaged to get closer to the top than ever before. Many of my friends who had looked upon me with a certain jealous satisfaction while I was going down looked upon me now as somewhat of an imposter as I was climbing back up.

I was deeply impressed by this dream, or whatever it was. And I believe it came true in my life by reason of my association with the liquor commission. I had established a good reputation I thought, for we had in the Granite Stake a very wonderful group of workers. Being released as president during a political controversy seemed to mark the bottom of the ladder for me; it was the low point in my career as a church man. After having been established as a stake president and having gone into the liquor commission not only with the consent of, but actually at the request of, President Grant, I felt that I had been wronged greatly so far as my reputation was concerned.

Next, however, came the beginning of the climb back: I moved to California for a time, where I thought I would take up my legal practice and then was called by the church authorities as president of the British Mission.

While president of the Granite Stake, I enjoyed some of the most interesting and impressive experiences of my life. We organized a prayer circle and met once each month in the Salt Lake Temple with the high council, the stake presidency, and the stake patriarch. Some very unusual spiritual experiences were had during that time, as well as in our high council meetings, our ward conferences, and in our stake conferences. We were among the leaders of the whole church in practically every activity upon which reports were made. It was a rich spiritual time for all of us.

Governor Blood appointed me to the liquor commission in 1935. Before accepting, I spoke to President Grant about it. He said, "By all means, we want you to take it, because we want the liquor controlled and not sold freely, and that will be your job." "Liquor *Control* Commission" was what he emphasized. I told President Grant that I did not want to take the job as I thought that not only would the people in my stake misunderstand, but the General Authorities as well. He said that he would make it right with them and spoke, I think, to a number of them. In any case, he came back to me the following week and said, "The Brethren are united in feeling that you should go to this liquor control commission work." I did so against my own better judgment and against the advice of my wife.

However, the appointment was only an interim appointment and needed to be confirmed by the Utah state senate. Because of the activities of a group of bootleggers and their agents against me, the senate refused to confirm the nominees, and, therefore, two years later, in 1937, I left the commission. Unfortunately, this turn of events left us up in the air. Shortly, however, I had an offer from a man living in Glendale, California, to trade his big home there for my home in Salt Lake City. We consummated the deal and moved to California in the spring of 1937.

Prior to the time when the Utah Senate refused to confirm my appointment to the liquor commission, President David O. McKay, who was now a counselor to President Grant, called me into his office and told me that the First Presidency had decided that I should be released as a stake president. He felt that it was inconsistent for a stake president to be chairman of the liquor commission. I told him that I would prefer to leave the liquor commission, since releasing me would, in a sense, hurt my standing in the community and that I did not wish to be released under those circumstances. President Grant heartily sustained me in this, but President McKay was adamant, and I think President J. Reuben Clark, President Grant's other counselor, supported him in this. Finally, they all decided to release me.

This was a discouraging blow as there had been some ugly rumors about my conduct as chairman of the state liquor commission. These rumors had been started by the bootleggers, whose products I had refused to stock in our stores. I was even offered bribes several times, including one for $25,000, to put their products on the list of preferred items. I told them that their products would never appear, and they never did. But because of this, enemies arose and in an underhanded way got word to the governor and the state senate that I was trafficking in this sort of thing. While the governor did not believe them, some members of the senate did, and when my name came up for confirmation, the senate refused. My associates and I consequently left the state liquor commission under something of a cloud.

This was one of the most trying times of my wife's and my life together. When faced with various requests to divide the stake, President Grant, who was always a firm friend of mine, affirmed, "As long as Hugh Brown is presiding he can handle the whole stake and there is no need of dividing it." But eventually the other brethren prevailed. Despite their having, in a sense, forsaken me in the storm, I did not in any way lose faith in the church as such, although I did have some reservations in sustaining some of the members of the First Presidency who had taken such an active part in getting me released from the stake presidency at such a crucial time. This was a period of heartbreak for both Zina and me.

During this period I recalled an incident that occurred while I was on my first mission, one that I related to my mother upon my return, and one that she said would be significant in my life. It was not a vision or a revelation but a strong impression, perhaps by way of a dream. I saw myself climbing a set of winding stairs and noticed a lot of other people. I got pretty close to the near crisis to bring the mariner's attention to the light—to make him appreciate its worth. I thank the Lord today for such a love to guide me and pray it may continue lest I stray. . . .

> Lots of love to all of you
> Yours always,
> Hugh

But for Zina's love and confidence and loyalty, I know that I should have yielded at times to discouragement and felt that nothing was worthwhile. Her love for me and mine for her and ours for the children has been the beacon which has kept alive a desire to carry on and make good. Now that we are grown old and the children have left us, this love has become the benediction of our years together. Ambition has cooled, desire for place or great wealth is gone. Life's richest treasures are ours, and some of the trials of the past have been for the purpose to help us to see real values.

I remained with the Deseret Mortuary Company until the Great Depression, when I became more interested in politics and made an unsuccessful bid for the Democratic nomination for the United States Senate. William H. King had filled this position for many years, and many local leaders of the party believed that he should no longer be there. However, my bid failed. Later, church president Heber J. Grant and Utah governor Henry H. Blood, together, persuaded me to take the chairmanship of the Utah State Liquor Control Commission.

Previous to my senatorial bid, I had been elected chairman of the state Democratic party. I resigned from this position to run for the senate. Those who encouraged me in the attempt were Henry D. Moyle, Calvin W. Rawlings, Delbert D. Draper, and a friend of Delbert—all stalwart Democrats. These men were very friendly with Governor Blood, who had just been elected to office. As a matter of fact, I gave the nominating speech for him at the state convention in Ogden. The other men who induced me to seek the nomination forsook the quest very shortly thereafter as political pressures were apparently brought to bear upon them, so that at the end I had only Draper, Rawlings, Moyle, and, I thought, Blood. Unfortunately, the event proved not only a fail-ure but disastrous in the sense that it weakened my standing in the minds of a great many people. For I was also at the time pres-ident of the Granite Stake, and many people thought that I should not be dabbling in politics while in that position.

Incidentally, the partners in the law firm where I worked, J. Reuben Clark, Preston Richards, and Albert Bowen, were all strong Republicans, although they did not interfere or give me advice one way or another as to my political activities. Still, I learned afterwards that they were all opposed to my running and were glad when I did not win. I broke with Clark, Richards, and Bowen at the beginning of the depression, I believe, when I was offered the position of attorney for the Home Owners Loan Cor-poration. I opened my own law practice and gave my whole time to the Home Owners' Loan work, which was not only remuner-ative but satisfying from the standpoint of service. After my sen-ate bid, I severed my relations so far as activity was concerned with the Democratic party, since it was at that time that I also became chairman of the state liquor commission.

During my time as chairman of the state Democratic party, I became quite well acquainted with Jim Farley, who was at the time the national Democratic party chairman and later Postmas-ter General of the United States. Through him I got to know President Franklin D. Roosevelt quite well, supported him in his bid for the presidency, and made it a point to see him whenever I was in Washington, D.C. I think these were the only two Dem-ocratic men with whom I ever became rather intimate.

Shortly after I came to Salt Lake City, I was called as a mem-ber of the Granite Stake presidency. At the time, Frank Y. Taylor was president. He first selected me as one of his counselors, and then a few months later I was appointed to replace him. There were 13,000 people in the stake, making it the largest stake in the church, and I think I only knew about one hundred of them. I was a bit uncertain as to how to proceed, since I did not know who would be good counselors. However, I'd gone to school with Marvin O. Ashton and also knew Stayner Richards. I selected Marvin as my first counselor and Stayner as my second coun-selor.

and fine and keep your mind bright and active so you may do the work He has for you.

I saw Zina yesterday and she is doing wonderful work out here. Everyone likes her because she is dependable and honest and genuine. I am proud of her just as I shall be proud of you when you are out in the mission field.

I hope you will have a very happy birthday and that each one will be better than the last. Lots of love and blessings.

Your devoted father
H. B. Brown

★ ★ ★ ★ ★

Seattle, Washington
Nov 9th, 1930

Dearest:-

Sunday is rather a lonely day when spent in a hotel with no friend or acquaintance near. Especially when the weather is overcast and dull and the view from one's window is limited by the fog, which in turn is the cause of almost continuous sounding of fog horns on the bay. Such is the physical environment in which I write you today. And physical environment does affect one's mental attitude.

However, I am rather bouyant mentally and spiritually which is attributed to a restful night's sleep after a long-distance phone conversation with the girl who has been the inspiration of my life for twenty years.

Strange how some incidents in one's life have so marked an influence. One may know that he is loved by another and be encouraged by that love, which is manifested by daily acts of devotion. But when a crisis comes and one is tempted to make a fool of himself, for no reason at all, and finds his mate ready to fight for him—this is a type of evidence of love with which one does not come in contact often—it is exhilarating and restores one's self-esteem, which has perhaps been gradually approaching the zero point. The feeling which most married men have sometimes—justifiable or not—that their importance is measured by their ability to anticipate and provide for the physical needs of a family is one of the most real and subtle enemies of self-respect.

To find, however, when a real test comes that someone cares enough to fight—not for the bread winner and debt payer alone—but for the lover—the boy friend, the companion of one's youth—this restores one's youthful fire and gives life its old time zest.

The above is especially true when forgiveness is spontaneous and permanent. One almost is glad the crisis came as it jars things back into their true perspective and restores the focus which is so often lost through too constant and continuous contact.

All of this reverie comes after seeing some shows and reading some recent magazine articles on the causes of divorce and the difficulty of keeping the matrimonial boat from running on the rocks. I thank the Lord daily for you and your precious love for me.

Last night I attended and wept thru Griffith's inspiring "talkie" Abraham Lincoln. It gives an intimate picture of him as a boy—a young man, beaten and buffeted by fate, of Ann Rutledge his first—and I believe his one real love—his heart broken, and battle with himself after her death, the other character-building episodes of his young manhood, all preparing him for the great mission which providence knew awaited him and for which he must be prepared by becoming acquainted with sorrow and disappointment and by overcoming difficulties.

His masterful handling of the most difficult situations in his mature manhood proves how thorough that preparation was. To me one of the most important parts of his training was the training of his heart which—filled with understanding and human sympathy as it was—often dictated to his master mind the way of right—which seemed to be opposed to the way of reason.

He could appreciate and make allowance for human weakness because he had been tempted to weakness himself and thus he understood.

The sustaining love of his early youth and the inspiration of that love called him back again and again when he would have given up in despair.

Such a love is like a beacon light in the darkness, and as I mentioned in the beginning of my letter—sometimes it takes a

Hugh B. Brown holding his first son, Hugh, after four daughters (ca. 1914).

The Brown family in Lethbridge, Alberta, Canada (ca. 1923). Back row, left to right: Zola, LaJune, Zina; front row: Hugh, Hugh C., Mary, Charles M., and Zina.

Hugh B. Brown by his army tent in Calgary, Canada, where he was attending an officer training course at military school.

The Hugh B. and Zina Card Brown family, with Zina Lydia and Zola Grace, in Cardston, Canada (ca. 1911).

Mormon missionaries in Norwich, England. Left to right: Henry A. Grover, George Webb, and Hugh B. Brown.

Hugh B. Brown (ca. 1906).

The Homer Manley and Lydia Jane Brown family (ca. 1885). Front row (left to right): Lily, Scott, Homer Sr., Hugh, Lydia, Lawrence, Homer Jr. (Bud); back row: Sarah Edna and Minnie. Seven more children would be born later.

Outside the Homer Manley and Lydia Jane Brown Lake Breeze home in Salt Lake City (ca. 1893). In the buggy are Nathan and Sarah Edna (Brown) Tanner with their new baby, N. Eldon Tanner (future counselor in the LDS first presidency). Lydia Jane Brown is beside the buggy; Homer Manley Brown is by the front porch. Hugh (with the dog) is seated in the grass by his brother Scott.

Zina Young Card at age fourteen.

Hugh B. Brown fishing in Alaska (ca. 1962).

Hugh B. Brown with some of the books from his library.

The first presidency of the LDS church in 1964: first counselor Hugh B. Brown, President David O. McKay, and second counselor N. Eldon Tanner.

Hugh and Zina Brown, June 1959.

The first presidency of the LDS church in 1961: President David O. McKay, first counselor Henry D. Moyle, and second counselor Hugh B. Brown.

The Brown family (ca. 1944). Front row, left to right: Hugh B., Zina C., and Mary B. and Edwin R. Firmage; back row: Zola B. Hodson, Margaret B. and Clinton O. Jorgenson, Carol B. Bunker, Zina B. Brown, Charles Manley and Grace B. Brown, and LaJune B. Munk.

The Quorum of the Twelve Apostles of the LDS church, April 1958. Front row, left to right: Joseph Fielding Smith, Harold B. Lee, Spencer W. Kimball, Ezra Taft Benson, Mark E. Petersen, and Henry D. Moyle; back row: Delbert L. Stapley, Marion G. Romney, LeGrand Richards, Richard L. Evans, George Q. Morris, and Hugh B. Brown.

The presidency of the Lethbridge stake of the LDS church: George W. Green, President Hugh B. Brown, and Asael E. Palmer.

Hugh B. Brown (ca. 1927).

The presidency and high council of the Granite stake, Salt Lake City, 1929–35. President Hugh B. Brown is seated in the middle.

Zina C. Brown and Hugh C. Brown (ca. 1940). Hugh C. Brown would be killed in action during World War II.

rather about the relationship to the Empire of the United States and Canada. (Incidentally, I spoke to seventy-five different Rotarian groups in and around London that year. They would advise ahead from group to group, and I was well, even enthusiastically, received.) At the close of this meeting, he asked me if I would come to his office in one of the suburbs of London to talk more about Salt Lake City and the Mormons. "I think there is going to be a war," he said. "If there is you will have to return to America and we may not meet again." I accepted his invitation.

As I sat down in his office, he said, "I have been greatly interested but also somewhat disturbed in what you have told me. You have told me that you believe that Joseph Smith was a prophet. You have said to me that you believe that God the Father and Jesus of Nazareth appeared to Joseph Smith. I cannot understand how a barrister and solicitor from Canada, a man trained in logic and evidence, could accept such absurd statements. What you tell me about Joseph Smith seems fantastic. I want to know more about the Mormon church. It would please me very much if you would prepare a brief on Mormonism and bring it here. Let me be the judge and you the attorney, and let's talk as lawyer to lawyer."

I replied that I did not need three days to prepare, that if he was ready, I would be ready to undertake the brief right then. He was somewhat surprised at my audacity, but when I told him that I had been teaching the gospel for nearly forty years he seemed to understand and said, "Let us then proceed."

I began by asking, "May I assume, sir, that you are a Christian?"

"I am."

"And that you believe in the Bible — the Old and New Testaments?"

"I do."

"Do you believe in prayer?"

"I do."

"You say that my belief that God spoke to a man in this age is fantastic and absurd?"

"To me, it is."

"Do you believe that God ever did speak to anyone?"

"Certainly, all through the Bible we have evidence of that."

"Do you believe that contact between God and man ceased when Jesus appeared on the earth?"

"No, such communication reached its climax, its apex, at that time."

"Do you believe that Jesus was the Son of God?"

"He was."

"Do you believe, sir, that after Jesus was resurrected, a certain lawyer, who was also a tentmaker, by the name of Saul of Tarsus, when on his way to Damascus, talked with Jesus of Nazareth, who had been crucified, resurrected, and had ascended into heaven?"

"I do."

"Whose voice did Saul hear?"

"It was the voice of Jesus Christ, for he so introduced himself."

"Then, my Lord, I submit to you in all seriousness that it was standard procedure in Bible times for God to talk to man."

"I think I will admit that, but it stopped shortly after the first century of the Christian era."

"Why do you say it stopped?"

"I can't say."

"There must be a reason. Can you give me a reason?"

"I do not know."

"May I suggest some possible reasons: perhaps God does not speak to man anymore because he cannot. He has lost the power."

"That would be blasphemous."

"Well, then, perhaps he doesn't speak to man because he doesn't love us anymore. He is no longer interested in the affairs of men."

"God loves all people, and he is no respecter of persons."

"Well, if he could speak, and if he loves us, then the only other possibility is that we don't need him. We have made such strides in science, and are so well educated, that we don't need God anymore."

Then he said, his voice trembling as he thought of impending war, "Mr. Brown, there never was a time in the history of the world when the voice of God was needed as it is now. Perhaps you can tell me why he doesn't speak."

1837. We went out to the spot, as nearly as we could tell, where they did their first baptizing in the River Ribble. There we held a meeting on the banks, which was well attended and quite inspirational. President J. Reuben Clark, of the First Presidency, spoke on this occasion, as did Joseph Anderson, President Grant, and Elder Richard R. Lyman, who was president of all the European missions of the church at that time. I also said a few words.

We met with a number of missionaries in Preston and had a meeting with them in the old cockpit of some fame in British Mormon history. We also visited the chapel that had been generously given out to the first missionaries in those early days.

Returning to London, we went to 5 Gordon Square, the headquarters of the British Mission. There, on the front steps, Joseph Cannon handed me the keys to the building and figuratively the keys to the British Mission.

Upon taking over the leadership of the mission, I soon found that an appointment had been made in Belfast, Ireland, for a meeting, and as President Cannon had left, I went to Belfast to fill that appointment.

I mention this meeting because it was one of the highlights of my mission. A large crowd had assembled in a rented building. In the crowd were ten young women who had become interested in the church. I seemed to have a special feeling for them and tried to preach to them the first principles of the gospel. At the close of the meeting all ten asked for baptism. Of course, the missionaries were delighted with this turn of events. The ten women were all later baptized, and all of them remained faithful to the church while I was in Britain. This marked a new high point in the Belfast Branch.

From there we went down to Dublin, which was quite different, both in spirit and in the quality of the people who were interested in the church. Very few converts had been made in Dublin, but those we had were staunch. However, in the whole of the Dublin Branch there was not one Irish member. All the members were German and were pig butchers. We had a rather large branch, enjoyed good meetings with the Saints, but received no response from the local people. The area, of course, was strongly Catholic.

I returned to London and took up the duties of the mission office. President Grant stayed on a few days and then bade us goodby. Without my family I felt somewhat lonely, but a great deal of work kept me rather busy.

My family — my wife, Zina, Manley, Margaret, and Carol — arrived by boat that September, and I drove down to South-hampton to meet them. Hugh had gone on ahead to attend a Boy Scout Jamboree in Holland and had returned to London before the rest of the family arrived. Hugh and I had some good times together in London. He was delighted to have been a member of this World Jamboree. He then went on to Scotland as a mission-ary, having been set apart before leaving Salt Lake City, and served the balance of his time there until war broke out.

During our first year we had sixty-two Elders and twelve sister missionaries in the British Mission. All of them were good, and, with only one exception, all made good later in their lives. The exception I need not mention further. Among those I remem-ber best were David S. King, later a member of Congress, Aldon J. Anderson, a district court judge, Emmett L. Brown, a practic-ing attorney in Salt Lake City, and Marvin J. Ashton, a member of the general superintendency of the Young Men's Mutual Improvement Association. These, and others, were outstanding missionaries, and we were all drawn together in a bond that has endured through the years. Some of them, known as the Gordon Square group, named after the address of the British Mission head-quarters, still meet together every month. We also meet twice a year at General Conference as a reunion of all the missionaries who labored in England during my presidency.

I had no counselors as mission president and had complete charge of the office. In addition, I was also editor and publisher of the *Latter-day Saints' Millennial Star* and wrote one article each week.

Just before the outbreak of war, in September 1939, I believe, I had occasion to become acquainted with a very prominent Englishman. I met him first on a golf course. Later, after I had spoken to a local chapter of the Rotary Club of which he was a member, he become interested in what I had to say. I was not speaking straight gospel at the time to that kind of crowd but

CHAPTER 6

BACK TO BRITAIN AND WORLD WAR II

In an attempt to pacify my turbulent feelings over having been released as president of the Granite Stake, the First Presidency called me to preside over the British Mission of the church shortly after I moved to California. I thereupon rented my new home there and left with President Heber J. Grant for England.

My home in California was large and even had five bathrooms. After receiving my call, I made arrangements to lease it for three years to a man who was an airline executive. Just one month after arriving in England, however, I received a cablegram that this man had shot and killed his wife and her lover on the piano bench in my front room, that he was going to jail, and that therefore my lease was broken.

Things go wrong sometimes for a period and then get worse, but there was only one thing to do and that was to carry on with chin up and try to keep a sense of humor. If this jealous husband had wanted to kill his wife you would think he might have taken her outside instead of mussing our front room, but we do not all do things the same way.

My brother was living in California at the time and, together with Preston Richards, my previous law partner, undertook to re-rent the house. Unfortunately, as people became aware that this was where a murder had taken place, no one wanted to rent it. I finally had to lease it for only $75 a month, whereas my original contract with the man from the airline was for $350 a month. Over the period of my assignment in England, this amounted to a terrific financial loss.

I left for England in June 1937 with President Grant and traveled with him throughout Europe for five weeks. My wife and family, including our children Hugh, Manley, Margaret, and Carol, joined me that September. Hugh had been set apart before he left Salt Lake City for a regular mission and labored in Scotland while we were in England.

While en route across the Atlantic Ocean, I wrote the following in my journal on June 27:

> This is the 29th anniversary of our wedding. We've been unusually happy and congenial. I've tried the patience of my loyal and devoted wife many times by my foolish side trips into politics and business, but she has stood by me and never complained. This is another evidence of the existence of God, for only God could have made such wise provisions for man's redemption as to give him a good wife.

The trip with President Grant was as memorable as any trip would be with a president of the church for any member of the church. We sailed from Montreal, Canada. There was quite a party of people from Utah on the boat, and some of them traveled with us on much of the journey. President Grant spoke at each meeting we held—in France, Belgium, Holland, and Germany—then back to England, where he took another trip to the Scandinavian countries and met with the Saints in Copenhagen. President Grant and party went on from there, and I returned to London. President Grant's talks were always inspiring to the people. Nothing of special importance occurred on the trip, but every day was a thrill to see the enthusiasm of the people in greeting the president of the church.

Shortly after arriving, I found myself greatly saddened at the faded glory of England and wrote in my journal,

> O for the power to show the English what could be done if they would establish athletic fields and teach proper diet; . . . above all, if they would return to religion, the integrating force which will hold the tottering world together if it is to be saved from wreck and ruin. How helpless I feel with these one hundred young men to try to bring help to this once-mighty nation. May God help us to find a way to bring the blessings of the gospel to some of them.

Upon returning to London, I met Joseph J. Cannon, the outgoing president of the British Mission. He, President Grant and party, and I then traveled to northern England and visited Preston, where the first Mormon missionaries to England had arrived in

Hugh B. Brown and grandson Edwin B. Firmage with Hubert H. Humphrey (ca. 1968).

The Homer Manley and Lydia Jane Brown family (ca. 1955). Back row, left to right: Romelia Hartley, Scott, Lawrence, Owen Gerold, and Zola Harris; front row: Winona, Edna Tanner, Homer, Lilly Anderson, Hugh, and Verona Hamblin.

My answer was, "He does speak. He has spoken, but people need faith to hear him."

We continued along these lines, compiling a profile of what a prophet would have to be like as we went, and at the end of the period he said, "Mr. Brown, I wonder if your people appreciate the import of your message. If what you have told me is true, it is the greatest message that has come to this earth since the angels announced the birth of Christ."

He then added, "I wish it were true. I hope it may be true. God knows it ought to be true. I would to God," he wept, "that some man could appear on earth and authoritatively say, 'Thus saith the Lord.' " Our meeting ended, and we were unable to ever meet again.

At the time, this gentleman was a member of Parliament, a member of the Supreme Court, a very prominent lawyer, author of many of the books which we used in Canada in our study of the law, and later a member of the House of Lords. I do not give his name because he was well-known in London and because his family knew nothing of his association with me. After I returned home, he became sufficiently interested in the gospel to request baptism. He wanted me to baptize him as soon as I returned to England. Unfortunately, it was several years before I could return, and he died in the meantime.

In retrospect, this was one of the outstanding experiences of my missionary career. Here was a man who was used to weighing evidence following an argument. He asked many searching questions, and we were together some three hours.

My contacts with the presiding brethren during this time were few and far between. We corresponded rather regularly, but as Elder Richard R. Lyman, a member of the Quorum of Twelve Apostles, was there presiding over all of the European missions, they felt it was not necessary to send visitors to Europe. We did have one visit from Elder Joseph Fielding Smith and his wife, Jessie Evans Smith. They toured the mission just before the war, and he was on the continent when war was finally declared. It was decided to have all the missionaries from all the European missions congregate in Copenhagen, Denmark, and arrange there for transportation home. However, as far as the British Mission was concerned, I had already taken precautions.

During the time we were in Europe, all the European mission presidents would occasionally meet in conference. For example, one conference was held in Copenhagen, another in Lucerne, Switzerland. And while we were traveling throughout the continent, Sister Brown and I, with the other mission presidents and their wives, listened to a lot of talk about war. I especially remember once riding on a train with a number of German officers. They were rather outspoken, almost insultingly so, speaking English for our benefit and explaining what was going to happen. I felt quite sure that war was not far away.

Upon returning to London afterwards, I immediately arranged with the United States Lines, the company with which the church did most of its transportation at the time, to hold for me one hundred berths to be called for as needed, probably all at one time. They agreed to do this, and the day the war broke out, when Neville Chamberlain, the British prime minister, announced that Britian was at war, I telephoned the shipping company and said I wanted those one hundred berths. They replied that ten thousand people were lined up there trying to get out, but they would honor their agreement. Accordingly, I sent for all the missionaries to come to London. We held meetings there for three days, waiting for the departure of the boat. Eventually, all of the missionaries left on that ship for home except five, who stayed with me for a time. The sister missionaries had gone on ahead, about thirty days in advance, because we were certain that war was coming and we wanted to protect them. Sister Brown and my family accompanied them.

Incidentally, the boat that preceded the one on which the elders went home was torpedoed in the Atlantic Ocean, and all of the crew and passengers were lost. It was an exciting time, and one which inspired deep humility, especially because I had taken it upon myself to put these elders on one boat.

The other missionaries of the European missions assembled in Copenhagen, according to arrangement, and were sent home as it became convenient. I stayed until February 1940 and then joined Thomas E. McKay in France. He was president of the

French-German Mission, as I think it was called at that time, with headquarters in Bern, Switzerland. He and two or three of his elders and I, with the balance of our group, sailed together and arrived home in late February. My family had temporarily rented a home in Salt Lake City, and shortly after arriving, I took them to southern California, where we lived again in Glendale.

In the meantime, the First Presidency had asked me to become coordinator for all LDS servicemen and to travel to most of the camps in the United States and Canada, trying to encourage the boys to be true to themselves and to the church during their military service. Just before taking up this work, I had again become associated with Charles S. Merrill with whom I had worked prior to going to England, and he asked me to come and take charge of his Ogden Mortuary, which I did, leaving my family in California. I stayed in the mortuary, had a room where I cooked my meals, and slept with the other dead people. It was a rather trying time.

On the morning of the Japanese raid on Pearl Harbor, I was holding a conference for servicemen in San Luis Obispo. When we learned of the attack, we knew, of course, that war would be immediately declared and that the status of these men in the service would change from preparatory training to active service.

There was a very strong feeling of despair. Many of the men felt despondent, because we were not prepared to enter into a war with Japan and Germany. The Japanese had made the initial attack and had destroyed much of our capacity to retaliate. Our losses were great both in terms of men and materiel, but my mission at the time was to try to bring hope, encouragement, and faith to the men, most of whom were very young. This, I am glad to say, was accomplished to some extent. I felt inspired beyond myself as I talked to the men, relating to them incidents from my own life that had helped and inspired me.

In the spring of 1942, I was traveling as coordinator somewhere in northern Montana when my wife Zina received a cablegram from the British war office saying that our oldest son, Hugh, who was a member of the Eagle Squadron of the Royal Air Force, had been reported missing in action. She was unable to get word to me for three harrowing days and suffered tremendously. I finally received notice when I arrived back in Salt Lake City and, of course, immediately went home to California. We clung to the slender hope that he might have escaped and was only missing, but three days later we received confirmation that Hugh had been "lost over the North Sea," which broke our hearts. His loss has been a source of sorrow to both Zina and me since that time. In fact, Zina keeps a rose, or some other blossom, by his picture, and recently we selected a burial spot for ourselves and others and have a marker there for him. Although his body is not there, it will remind us of our son who gave his life for country and church.

When old men are killed in battle, it just means that the natural processes are being helped along a little, but seeing young men go whose life has hardly started seems terribly wrong. Still, if Hugh had been given a choice of exits, he would have taken this one. He was at the wheel of his plane on scout work, not fighting or trying to kill, but defending the British people whom he loved. He was in good health, and he flew into eternity with the smile for which we will all remember him. He had had an unusually full life for one so young. Always adventurous, he is now experiencing the greatest adventure of all. I am sure he is going on with his education and experience under conditions far better than any he knew here. His schooling, his scouting, his extensive travel, his mission, his college, his work on the farm and in the store, his flying school, and finally his training as an officer in the famous R.A.F. constitute a fuller and richer life than that enjoyed by many men who stay on earth for eighty years. Through it all, he went to meet the Savior with a clean record and a pure life. God be thanked for such a son, brother, and pal.

My last letter to him follows:

Mar. 10 — 42

My Dear Son Hugh:

Until you are a father and get letters from your son you cannot know what such a letter as yours of Feb 12 + 14 means to me. The sentiments you express, the ideals you are upholding, the ambitions you have, the zest for life, and the urge for more abundant living — your faith and love and loyalty — these things make a father feel that regardless of his own limitations, when he has a son to carry on—starting as it were from his shoulders and destined for far greater things than he has been able to do—a father feels that life could have given him no greater blessing. One comes to realize why God in blessing the patriarchs of old gave them as a crowning blessing the promise of a noble and worthy posterity. God bless you, my son. No father ever loved his son more than I do you.

Unless you go through a similar experience, you will never know what I felt and could not say that day at the train station in Salt Lake City when you left so confidently and carefree for what I knew was to be a harrowing experience. It was as a Gethsemane to me. Not that I would have prevented you from going, but that I would have spared you the danger and have gone myself instead. I am able to read much between the lines in your letters and know from experience that you are living more in a month than one does in a year of the soft and sometimes effortless lives of peace time, school time, love time, spring time, and life at home.

I am with the soldiers daily, as you know, and have my heart-to-heart talks with them, and though they here know nothing of the "real thing," still the fact that they are to go and that no longer can they direct their own lives or follow their chosen courses has a sobering effect, and they mature so fast that the change is plainly seen from one visit to the next. What a shame that so many of them will have to finish in another sphere what they now hope to accomplish here. I think I'm not pessimistic, but I know too well that war plays no favorites.

As for you, Hugh, I feel and have always felt that you are to be spared, not because He loves you more than others, but that you have a great work to do after the war—you must carry on where I leave off. Knowing this it makes me shed tears of joy and pride when you write me that you are not allowing the environment of war to undermine your manhood, to rob you of your self-respect which is the cement of character, or to unfit you for the great work you are to do in the new world which must be built after this present one is well nigh destroyed.

Everywhere I go I meet friends who know you, and always they ask of you and send love. Last Sunday, I took mother and Chuck and the girls and drove to San Diego to attend a stake conference. We have a large number of LDS men there in the army, navy, and air force, and they seem to appreciate our visits. Wilford Woolf, of Provo, is there and sent love and greetings. His brother Anthony is in a camp in Texas. Thornton Booth is still in Ft. Lewis, Washington, but is, I think, booked to sail this month. Scott Clawson is in one of the air training camps in Georgia. We tried to find Wes McDonald in San Diego but could not locate him.

I am leaving today for San Francisco, Portland, Seattle, Spokane, Butte, and Salt Lake City, so will be gone about two weeks. Mother has written you regarding my trip to Texas. It was good to see LaJune and the kiddies. They are doing pretty well there, but it is not a place to make a permanent home. Zina and Garr are very happy—she is still working and he expects to be called soon to some branch of military service. Manley is just now waiting for word regarding his next flying course and is impatient to get at it.

I am glad to get word of church activities there. I really feel that I should return there and take over the mission and at the same time act as sort of chaplain for the LDS boys who are there. It has never seemed right to me for us to leave those people without help from experienced men from headquarters. That may happen yet. It would be great to meet you there.

We are waiting for the next Saturday *Deseret News*, as last week's issue told of your article which is to appear March 14th.

Well, son, I have written at great length and rather ramblingly, but it is so good to have a real chat with you. After reading your fine letter which came this a.m., I just had to sit down to write you before leaving for the north.

Cling to your ideals, my son, keep your faith in God and in yourself and your future, and you'll come through O.K. I do hope the Canadian position develops. I'd be so proud to have you instructing in my old stomping ground.

> Love and blessings from your devoted father,
> Hugh B. Brown

Soon after Hugh's death, the call came to me to return to England. I, of course, could not take my family and went alone. I flew first to New York City, where I had been told I would receive my instructions. Upon arrival I was told to take a certain boat at a certain place—a small boat which would take me to the larger vessel in which I was to travel. We went out to the boat and climbed the Jacob's Ladder to get in. (There was one other passenger, a major in the Dutch army.)

When we stepped onto the deck, we were met by the captain who asked, "What are you doing here?" We told him of our assignment and showed him our papers. He said, "I have absolutely no place to put you. This is not a passenger vessel. It is a freight boat. You will have to put up with what we can do for you." He thereupon ordered members of his crew to clear out the room which was used for medicine and doctors and to make it available to us, to put in a bunk bed which the two of us used all the way over. The odor and aroma from the various medicines, including carbolic acid, plagued us throughout the whole of the trip.

I think this was unquestionably the roughest boat trip I ever had. It took us seventeen days. There were sixty-two vessels in our convoy, and we were guarded by several torpedo boat destroyers. The heaviest storms I ever witnessed on the ocean, and I have crossed it fourteen times, were encountered just off the banks of Nova Scotia. One of the vessels in our convoy broke in two. I was standing on the deck at the time it separated. However, being a liberty ship, it was built in such a way that each half of the vessel remained afloat and was salvaged, together with all the people on it.

We docked at a secret landing just off the coast of Wales, and as we had been accompanied by enemy submarines most of the time, we were glad to see shore. I went on into London and took over the affairs of the mission from Andre K. Anastasiou, with whom I had left the affairs of the mission and whom I had appointed acting mission president when I left. I had no family with me, no missionaries. It was a rather lonely assignment. But in addition to my missionary labors, I was still coordinator for all LDS servicemen and did quite a lot of traveling in this connection. Fortunately, this helped to take up my time.

While acting as coordinator, I sent a telegram one Saturday evening to the head chaplain of a camp near Liverpool. I told him that I would be in his camp the following morning at 10 o'clock and would like to meet with all the Mormon servicemen.

The next morning, upon arrival, I was met by seventy-five servicemen all in uniform. They seemed glad to see me as I represented to them something of home. Then the chaplain to whom I had sent the telegram stepped forward and introduced himself. He said, "I want to congratulate you. Although I did not receive your telegram until yesterday telling me of your arrival and the meeting you proposed to hold this morning, upon receipt I got in touch with the various officers and units in camp and found that there are seventy-six Mormon boys serving here. Seventy-five of them are here this morning. What method do you pursue to accomplish such unusual results?"

I told him if he would come into our meeting he probably would get a good idea of how we proceeded. He expressed some surprise at me inviting him to attend our meeting but gladly accepted. We went to the camp, took over a quonset hut, and assembled our forces.

Upon assembling, I asked the men present how many of them had been on missions. Fully 50 percent of them raised their hands. I then designated six of them to come up and prepare and administer the sacrament. I appointed another six to sit on the opposite side of the stand and be prepared to speak. I looked at my minister friend, who was sitting on my right hand, and found he had his mouth open with surprise and amazement that I had the audacity to call young men out of a military unit to become suddenly ministers of the gospel.

I then asked what they would like to sing, and almost with one voice they replied, "Come, Come Ye Saints." I asked if anyone present had ever led the music, and again over 50 percent of them raised their hands. I selected one of them to take charge of the singing and asked if anyone could play a portable organ. A good percentage of them had had some experience in that field, and I appointed one to play the organ.

We had no books, we had no leaflets or anything else to refer to for the words of the hymn, but those young men sang the four verses of "Come, Come Ye Saints" without a quiver. The last verse was most inspiring. The words here begin "And should we die before our journey's through, Happy Day, All is Well" and were sung with a verve, an enthusiasm, a dedication, and a resignation that was indeed moving. I looked at the man at my right and found him weeping, and I joined him.

After the hymn and the opening prayer, I asked one of the men at the sacrament table to offer the blessing on the bread. The young man knelt at the table and began the blessing with the words, "O God, the Eternal Father, . . ." but then paused for what I am sure was a full minute before proceeding.

After the meeting I found this young man, put my arm around his shoulder, and asked, "Son, is something troubling you?"

He replied, "Why, sir?"

I said, "You seemed to have trouble in giving the blessing on the bread. Why did you pause so long?"

He answered, "Well, sir, it's like this. Just a few hours before the meeting, I was over France and Germany on a bombing mission. We had made our run, deposited our bombs, and gained altitude, preparatory to returning to England across the channel. We suddenly ran into heavy flak. Part of the tail assembly was shot away from our plane. One of my engines was out. Several of my crew were sounded out for their opinion. It looked hopeless. There we were over enemy territory with a crippled plane which seemed at the time to be unable to get back across the channel. We had the choice of landing in the channel or behind enemy lines and being taken prisoners.

"At that moment I remembered what my mother had told me and what I learned in Sunday school, seminary, and other church meetings. According to my mother, 'My boy, if at any time you find youself in a situation where men cannot help you, call upon God and he'll hear your prayer.' Surely this was a case where men could not help me. It looked like a hopeless proposition to think that any power could see us back across the channel in a plane so badly damaged, but I thought it only fair to put it to the test. Accordingly, I cried out from the cockpit, 'O God, the

Eternal Father,' and then I asked him to sustain that ship in the air until it returned across the channel.

"Brother Brown," he continued, "that is exactly what he did. We were able to come back to England and to land at this airfield here, just outside of Liverpool. Upon landing, I learned of this meeting and ran all the way to get here. As you can see I haven't changed my battle dress. But when I knelt at the table and pronounced his name again it occurred to me that I had not stopped to say 'Thank you,' and my conscience bothered me on that. I had to pause in the blessing on the bread and under my breath to thank the Lord for his miraculous help in saving us from what looked to be either death in the channel or a long term as prisoners in an enemy camp. That's why I paused during the blessing."

Well, we went on with our meeting. We had these six young men speak, each of whom spoke with power and conviction. It was thrilling to see young beardless boys defend the truth, bearing witness of its divinity. My friend, the minister, wept most of the time as he listened to these young men say, "I know that God lives, that man is immortal, that death does not end conscious existence." Each of them said in his own way that he had this conviction and that he was therefore not afraid to face death if required to do so.

After these young men had spoken, I looked at the clock and saw that it was nearly noon. I said to the men, "It is time now for chow. We'll have to dismiss this meeting or you will miss your meal." Again, with one voice, they spoke out, "We can eat army grub any time. Let's hold a testimony meeting." I said, "Well, fellows, if you hold a testimony meeting you will be here another two hours on top of the two hours we have already spent." They replied, "That is our wish."

I turned to my friend and said, "I am sure this is an experience not common to you in your own church. If you would prefer, we would be glad to excuse you and let you go."

He put his hand on my knee and answered, "Sir, I would like to stay if you will permit it." Of course, I invited him to stay.

From then on I was simply a referee as the boys were rising eight and ten at a time in various parts of the hall, until all seventy-five had spoken. They bore their testimonies, they thanked God for the privilege of serving their country, for their homes and their families which gave them the faith to endure the great stress and strain of military life in active warfare.

At the close of the meeting, when all had spoken and we had dismissed, my friend turned to me and said, "Sir, I have been a minister of the gospel for twenty-one years, but this has been the most unusual and inspiring event in my ministry. I have never witnessed anything like this in my life. Tell me how do you do it? How did you know which of these young men to call upon? How could you remember them all?"

When I assured him that I had not met any of those men, he again expressed great surprise. He said, "I have 600 men from my church in this camp and if I should call on them, even after giving them notice, they would not respond as your men have done."

During this time we had some other rather interesting, though a bit dangerous, experiences. London had been under heavy siege and the bombing had been terrific. Many of the buildings around our headquarters were ruined. Our offices at 5 Gordon Square had been bombed out, and the mission headquarters had been removed to Ravenslea, in southwest London, at 149 Nightingale Lane.

One day I was in the back yard of the mission headquarters at Ravenslea and heard the noise of what seemed to be a plane. When it got to within a certain distance from our place, which was just three blocks from a railway center, I noticed the power was suddenly cut off, and it dove to the earth and struck just a few blocks away, completely destroying fifteen houses. When I heard the sound of the engines being cut off, I was sure what was happening. And, as I have a great affinity for the earth, I lay down on the ground. The explosion broke every window in Ravenslea.

After the explosion I arose from the garden and tried to go into the house, but the explosion had expanded the doors and we had to break them down to get in. When I finally got in, I found Sister Dunn and some of the young women from the local church huddled in one room off the kitchen. They had not been able to get out because the doors had been jammed shut. We finally got through and let them out. Brothers Norman Dunn and Alvin Gittins, a local missionary, were in the office at the time. Both of them were under the table when I went in. We consequently moved the mission offices to Birmingham.

I might add here that I had earlier met a young woman before leaving England at the time of the outbreak of war and told her that I would be back and baptize her later on. Upon my arrival the second time, I went up to Birmingham to hold a conference and she came to the stand and reminded me of my promise. She said she was ready for baptism. It was my pleasure to baptize her, and she later became the wife of Alvin Gittins. Although his parents were opposed to the marriage, they were very much in love. I married them and made arrangements for them to come to Utah and attend Brigham Young University in Provo. Subsequently, they both left the church. Since then, Alvin Gittins made quite a name for himself as a portrait painter.

While we were living in Birmingham I again suffered a severe attack of the tic douloureux. I immediately got in touch with the First Presidency, who ordered me to return home for medical attention. However, this being the height of the war, there was no possibility of getting transportation, so I made my way to the head surgeon of the British Army. Having been an officer in the Canadian army, I had entree to this man. When I got to his office and told him what my trouble was, he exclaimed with the emphasis of an oath, "If you've got that, we're going to get you home, no matter what! My wife suffered for years with the tic douloureux, and I know what it is."

He thereupon arranged for me to fly to Scotland, where I took passage on what turned out to be a freight ship. I sat on a nail keg all the way home, suffering agonizing pain from the tic. I arrived in Washington, D.C., where I was met by Victor L. Brown, a nephew. I was very glad to go with him to his home, to have a bath, and to get a little rest. Then I caught a plane home and, shortly after arriving, was operated on for the tic.

Two weeks later, and although the doctor recommended at least three more months' rest, I caught a plane for England. This proved to be unwise, and the pain eventually became more severe than ever. Unfortunately, I was not able to have this resolved until two or three years later.

After the close of the war, in September 1945 I believe, my family, including my wife, Margaret, and Carol, joined me again in England. Margaret served as a missionary during this term, and I was glad to welcome my wife and other children as well. Manley, who had married, was living in New York City. We stayed in London until 1946, when I was released and Selvoy J. Boyer succeeded me as president.

One of the things that was particularly detrimental to the members of the church in Britain during my absence was a return to sectarian methods of procedure and doctrine. I found, for instance, that a lot of things had been carried over from the preconversion days of many members. In fact, the whole mission seemed to be moving toward apostasy. Although quite a number of the Saints left the church during the war, we were able to re-establish most of them. This was not the fault of the mission president, however, who faced insurmontable problems during the war: no Elders, no real leaders, and no seasoned members.

Shortly before I returned home, a man came into my office in London. This man was an ex-army officer from India. He said, "I am the diplomatic correspondent for *The People*. My employers have asked me to write a series of articles against the Mormons. I thought it only fair to come to you and talk about it before starting those articles."

I asked, "You say you are going to write against the church?"

"I certainly am. What I am going to write will not be good, will not be favorable."

"It is interesting that you know enough about the Mormons to write authoritatively about them. Would you mind telling me just what you know?"

"Not a darned thing."

"Wouldn't you like to know something about the Mormons?"

"Yes, I really would."

I told him that we had the best library in Europe on the Mormon question. "Everything that has ever been written against us is there—and all the things that have been written in favor of the church, all the works by church leaders are there."

"I'll do just that. I'll spend thirty days," as he said, "plugging up on Mormonism."

I thought it only fair to warn him that if he spent thirty days in that library reading on Mormonism, he would ask for baptism. When I told him that he said a lot of things I probably should not repeat. "Why," he said, "the idea that I would become a Mormon is preposterous!"

I answered, "I thought it only right to tell you that's what is going to happen to you. When you come out you will ask for baptism."

He went into the library; he read and studied; and, as he afterwards told me, he prayed. I returned home in the meantime and was teaching at Brigham Young University when I received a cable—less than thirty days after our interview. The cable was brief but to the point. It said, "I think you will be interested to know that I am being baptized next Friday."

We stayed in England until the spring of 1946. I had earlier received word that I might be asked to go to Brigham Young University as coordinator of some 2,000 LDS boys who had returned home from the service. Many of them were in a state of near apostasy because of what they had seen and heard in military service. They had difficulty in harmonizing the idea of God with what they had seen, especially those who had been in Germany and had seen the atrocious things that were done during the war.

Upon returning home, I made my report, but as I had very little legal experience in United States law, I found it difficult to make any headway. Soon, however, I was asked by the brethren to go to Brigham Young University as servicemen's coordinator and try to re-establish the faith of these young veterans. I took my family, found a home in Provo, and moved there in 1946. I became a professor, taught political science for some time, but gradually worked into teaching gospel subjects full time in the department of religion. We had great success in that field; people wanted to get into my classes for some reason, and when I left, I had moved into the largest classroom they had—the auditorium in the Joseph Smith Memorial Building—where I had 600 students. It was supposed to be a simple lecture program, I presume. But I enjoyed it, and my students seemed to profit from it.

After starting at BYU, I experienced increased attacks from the tic douloureux. So I soon left for the Mayo Clinic in Rochester, Minnesota, where I received the best of attention. My son Manley accompanied me on the journey east but did not stay long as he was a student at the University of Utah and could not afford to miss too many of his classes. He arranged for my wife to come to Rochester, and she stayed with me the balance of the time. This operation differed from the former of two years earlier in that the surgeons took out a section of nerve instead of just severing it. Unfortunately, this left that side of my head completely numb, and this is the way it will have to stay until I leave this vale of existence. Still, this has not been nearly as distressing as the pain. I returned to BYU and remained there until 1950.

CHAPTER 7

THE CALL TO SALT LAKE CITY

After World War II, while teaching at BYU, I was earning a yearly compensation of $4,500. I had had thirteen years of non-remunerative employment in the church as coordinator for LDS servicemen, president of the British Mission, and other callings, so $4,500 was an improvement.

Early one morning in the spring of 1950, I received a telephone call from a man based in Toronto, Ontario, Canada. He said, "I represent a large oil company in Houston, Texas. We are moving into Alberta where they have recently discovered oil. We want to incorporate a company and try to develop some oil fields. We want a man who has practiced law in Canada and in the United States, and you have been recommended to us. I am phoning to ask if you will be available to come to Alberta and join our firm, to incorporate our company, and to become our general counsel."

I replied that I could not leave because I was teaching at the university. He answered, "I don't know what you are getting at the university, but whatever it is I will multiply it by ten if you will come." This seemed to be more than I could resist, and I went immediately to Salt Lake City to meet with members of the First Presidency. I told them of the offer. They said, "By all means, go!" Upon their recommendation, I left for Canada in 1950.

The man from the oil company not only kept his promise to multiply what I was making by ten, but he also multiplied it by twenty before I got through. This development resulted in my financial emancipation. I had had mortgages on my home and had been heavily in debt. I had a large family, some of whom were still in school. Thus, this offer of employment came as a great blessing to me, for although we did not discover oil, I became a manager as well as general counsel. The salary I received my first year amounted to more than $100,000, relieving me from the bondage of debt.

In October 1953, I was up in the Canadian Rockies, supervising the drilling of an oil well. Although my family was in good health and good spirits and I was making good money, more than ever before, I was deeply depressed and worried and could not understand why. Early one morning I went up into the mountains and talked with the Lord in prayer. I said to him, "It is apparent that I am going to become a millionaire. I pray thee, O Lord, not to let it happen if it will be detrimental to me or to my family."

That night I drove from the camp back down to Edmonton, still spiritually disturbed and depressed. Without having dinner that night, I went into the bedroom by myself, telling my wife that she should stay in the other room, as I felt I would not have a good night's rest. All night long I wrestled with the spirit of wishing that I could be rubbed out of existence. I had no thought of suicide but wished the Lord would provide a way for me to cease to be. It was terrible. The room was full of darkness, you could almost feel it, and the evil spirit that prevailed was so real that I was almost consumed by it.

About three o'clock in the morning, I was barely able to call to my wife. She came in and asked me what was the matter. Upon closing the door, she said, "Oh, Hugh, what's in this room?" I replied, "The devil." We spent the balance of the night together, much of it on our knees, but we were not relieved. The next morning, I went to the office knowing that no one would be there because it was a Saturday. I again knelt in prayer and asked for deliverance from this evil spirit. I then felt for the first time a peaceful spirit come over me. I telephoned my wife to tell her that the spirit of darkness had been dispelled, that the depression was ended.

That night while I was taking a bath about ten o'clock the telephone rang. My wife answered and called to me. "Salt Lake City is calling," she said. I was somewhat perturbed at being called at that time of night. Upon going to the phone, I heard a voice say, "This is David O. McKay calling. The Lord wants you to spend the balance of your life in the service of the church. The

Council of Twelve Apostles has just voted that you should take the place made vacant by the recent death of Brother Stayner Richards, and you are to become an assistant to the Twelve Apostles. Can you be here tomorrow to be sustained during the morning session of General Conference?" I was greatly astonished. I told him that I could not come at that time, since there were no planes flying, but that I would come as soon as I could.

Shortly after I arrived in Salt Lake City that fall, I met with President McKay in his office, where he and his first counselor Stephen L Richards were meeting. We discussed together the duties that would soon descend upon me. Then President McKay was mouth in setting me apart as an assistant to the Council of the Twelve Apostles. I was greatly impressed by President McKay as a man, and also by President Richards. They reviewed for me some of their own experiences and previewed what I might expect in my labors in the ministry.

During our meeting, I told President McKay of my experience of depression prior to my calling. He said that, in his opinion, practically every one of the General Authorities of the church had encountered some comparable experience. That is, each of them was tested mightily before he was taken into the service. President McKay also told me that if I would be true and faithful, there were other callings lying ahead for me. He did not specify what he meant at this time but indicated that later on I would be asked to assume greater responsibilities.

We purchased a house at 117 Alpine Place, just off 900 South and Gilmer Drive, in the city, where we moved in December 1954. We lived there until we later moved into the Eagle Gate Apartments, where we remained about one year and then moved to what was to be our home for the remainder of our lives—1002 Douglas Street.

Before continuing, I believe I should mention several incidents that preceded my calling so that the record might be complete. In about 1901, while we were living at Spring Coulee, all of the visitors to the conferences of the Alberta Stake came to our place en route to Cardston and usually stayed over night.

One time Francis M. Lyman, president of the Quorum of Twelve Apostles, came to our house. He spoke in our stake conference the next day, and on our way home afterwards Mother told me of an experience she had had while President Lyman had been talking. She said, "As I looked upon him he ceased to be Francis M. Lyman and became Hugh B. Brown, and I saw you as occupying the position he then held. I know as I know I live that that's what's going to happen to you, and if you will just behave yourself and do what is right, the time will come when you will be called into the Council of the Twelve Apostles."

Several years later, and shortly before leaving for my first mission to England, I received a patriarchal blessing from John Smith, the Presiding Patriarch to the Church, on 26 January 1904. In it I was told, "Thou shalt be wise in counsel among thy brethren and valiant in the defense of truth, virtue, and righteousness. Thou shalt travel much at home and abroad, laboring in the ministry, and thy voice shall be heard among the nations of the earth, proclaiming the words of life and salvation unto all who shall listen. And when necessary thou shalt prophesy, for thy guardian angel will often whisper in thine ear and open the eyes of thine understanding." At the time, I did not interpret this blessing to mean that I would become one of the General Authorities, but afterwards Patriarch Smith said to me, "Young man, you will someday sit among the highest councils in the church."

The following year in 1905 while I was in England, Elder Heber J. Grant held a large meeting of all the missionaries in the British Isles. Toward the close of the meeting he said, "Brethren, I feel inspired to say to you that there is someone here who will someday become a member of the Council of the Twelve." I did not think that applied to me, but as it turned out, I was the one Elder Grant seemingly beheld in vision. For he told me in later years that he had wanted to appoint me to the Twelve after I had chaired the Utah State Liquor Commission but that some of the brethren had opposed it, fearing adverse criticism.

Finally, following my mission, I received a second patriarchal blessing. This one, pronounced by Henry L. Hirman, is dated 19 March 1907 and read much like the first: "As thou growest in years, thou may grow in strength and in power to serve God and keep his commandments and to be useful in his hands in spreading the Gospel and assisting to redeem Zion that the way may be prepared for the coming of the Savior . . . And thy labors shall be crowned with success, for thou shalt have the privilege of associating with heavenly beings in thy labors. And then thou shalt receive new inspiration in thy labors in behalf of the youth of Zion, in spreading the Gospel and gathering Israel. . . . Be thou obedient to the Priesthood that is sent to preside over thee, and thou wilt be raised to full feature of honor and of truth in the midst of the people that will make thee mighty."

In reflecting upon these and other events, I am convinced that they, together with the prophetic understanding of my mother, seemed to set me apart as one who had been chosen to be one of the General Authorities someday.

As I have mentioned, I was most impressed during my first meeting with the First Presidency in 1953 and later with members of the Council of Twelve Apostles by their complete dedication to the work and by the sincerity with which they extended the hand of fellowship to me as a newcomer. Although I have had some rather difficult experiences since I became a General Authority by reason of some misunderstandings and disagreements, it has been a truly wonderful experience.

At the time of my calling in 1953, I felt that I had cut the line between the past and the future in that I would now be required to give my whole time to the church. Previously, I had divided my time between my law practice, business ventures, and church work as a stake president, but now the church work would come first. I visited a great many of the stakes between the time of my appointment and my subsequent call to the Council of Twelve Apostles.

As an assistant, my duties consisted largely of attending and presiding over quarterly stake conferences, ordaining and setting apart local officers in various capacities, officiating in temple marriage ceremonies and sealings, and in other ways assisting the members of the Council of Twelve Apostles. Mine was a calling I tried to undertake with humility and deep gratitude, despite some misgivings.

115

There were many inspiring experiences in my travels among the peoples of the stakes. I was impressed, first, by the sincerity with which they received me, by the enthusiasm which they showed in connection with my assignment, and by their interest in my attempts to teach them the gospel of Jesus Christ.

As we would go into the stakes we were invariably met by the stake presidency at the airport or the train depot. They were most considerate and honored the office we held. This made me feel very humble. I can now recall a number of such experiences as I think back on those days when we administered to the sick, gave blessings to the despondent, and advised the uncertain and the insecure regarding the course they should take in order to reap the blessings of permanent association with the Saints in the hereafter. These experiences required us to exercise the spiritual insight which, I am glad to say, came on many occasions with exceptional force — not only to me but to those with whom I was associated. Most of the time I traveled alone. That is, we did not go in pairs as the growth of the church made it impossible for us to cover the stakes by twos.

About one year after I came down from Canada, President McKay called me into his office and said, "We have a number of applications from married people for cancellation of their temple sealings. This involves inquiry into the causes and results of civil divorce. I would like you to take this assignment over, if you will. Investigate all these cases and with your legal background advise me as to what should be done in each case."

Elder Albert E. Bowen had partially fulfilled this position previously, and later Elder Matthew Cowley. Elder Cowley did a remarkable job but had to call in help to do much of the detail work which was involved. When I took it over I called in an extra secretary and gave it a great deal of my time between stake conferences. During that assignment, I must have processed several hundred cases where applications had been made for the cancellation of temple sealings. These were usually granted if there was sufficient evidence of infidelity on the part of either of the parties involved or if there was conclusive evidence that there was no hope of reconciliation.

One of the first things I did was to ask President McKay to advise me as to the grounds for divorce and as to what I was to look for in my investigations before making my recommendations to him. He explained that the initial reason for a temple cancellation was immorality on the part of either the husband or wife, but that this was not the only reason. He noted that "where a couple had learned that they could not live together, where they had obtained a civil divorce and had married again (sometimes in the temple, which should not have been done and consequently had to be corrected), and especially where there were no children involved, a cancellation should be granted."

In those instances where a divorced man or woman had been remarried in the temple without first having been granted a cancellation of temple sealing, we very often would immediately authorize a cancellation of the first sealing. Sometimes we found ourselves in a position where the woman who had the civil divorce had been permitted to go to the temple to be sealed to another man. This meant, in effect, that she was sealed to two men. President McKay required that in all future cases a woman could not be sealed to another man until there was first a cancellation of the former sealing. (Of course, the doctrine of a plurality of wives allows for the possibility of more than one wife being sealed to one husband in the hereafter.)

As time went on we established rules by which we were later guided as to how to proceed in investigating these cases. For example, I made it a rule to call in the parties concerned or to visit them during a stake conference in their own area. I would get them together and talk to them together, then separately, and try to find out the reason for their civil divorce. I found that this kind of investigation frequently resulted in reconciliation, especially if there had been no intervening marriage of either of the parties.

I also counseled with a lot of men and women who were simply contemplating a civil divorce. Most of them had not yet come to the point where they were thinking seriously about a cancellation of their temple sealing, but where they had formed alliances with other people and were contemplating divorce. I found it helpful to go over the history of their past married life, to investigate their claims against their spouse, usually incompatiblity, and then in many cases to try to bring about a reconciliation.

Frequently, the parties concerned had accused each other of things of which they were not guilty. There were often incidents of cruelty—sometimes extreme cruelty, sometimes neglect, but always one or the other party had cause for action. In getting into the details of their marital troubles, I usually found that a breakdown of communication was at the root of their problems.

They would get to a point where they would not speak to each other for months at a time. Of course, living together as husband and wife and not communicating created an impossible impasse. It was in cases like these that I believe I was most effective—getting each party to understand that he or she was not wholly innocent.

In terms of the causes of divorce among church members I would rank the most significant as infidelity on the part of one or the other spouse. Then, of course, cruelty to various degrees. Then, a lack of understanding, especially regarding financial matters. Many men, I found, refused to give their wives any money of their own, were selfish in distributing joint funds, and wanted to make their wives slaves of the family. Sexual difficulties were also one of the chief problems of unhappiness and divorce.

It is regrettable that we do not have better programs of sexual education in Mormon families. We have a very strict rule of conduct and where a husband or wife does not live up to that rule, the other is likely to seek separation or divorce. A certain flexibility is required in all of these cases, and this is what I tried to keep in mind as I proceeded with my assignment.

During the several years I was employed in this capacity, President McKay never refused or failed to concur in my recommendations. I realize that I may be patting myself on the back a little, but acting under his instructions and guidelines, I was able to weed out those that should not be considered and present to him only those that qualified for divorce under his rules.

Often during those years of service, I referred the parties to psychiatrists and psychologists, many of whom were members of the church, who were very helpful in getting to the facts, advising the parties concerned, and bringing about a reconciliation. I was glad to get the help of professionals in that capacity.

In approaching marriage, all of us need to overcome our native selfishness, our desire to have what we want regardless of its effect upon others. This includes arrogance, lack of consideration for the other party, and extreme stinginess on the part of many men who "earn all the money." Wives often give twenty-four hours a day to their families, preparing their meals, and keeping their homes in order, while their husbands go to work in the morning and come home in the evening. Very often the husband is so absorbed in the work of his office that when he gets home he is not communicative. He wants to hide behind a paper or a book and leave his wife out of his home life. Much of the burden of rearing a family is left, by many men, to the mother.

It presents difficult problems when husbands and wives disagree with one another. In my own life my wife has upheld and sustained me in decisions I have felt I have had to make for the benefit of the family. I have always tried to discuss these decisions with her fully. Her advice and intuition have invariably helped me to make the right decision. The answer to problems is usually a reformation of behavior and attitudes on the part of spouses. It is never easy, but it can be done.

It is a dangerous thing to try to regulate the private lives of husbands and wives or for church leaders to go into the bedroom of a couple who are married and try to dictate what they should or should not do. Many of the problems people bring to the authorities of the church should be settled by the persons themselves. They know the basic rule of right and wrong. For example, there are cases where abortion is absolutely justified, in fact necessary, such as in the case of forcible rape, the threat of permanent injury to the mother's health or life, or the possibility of a grossly deformed birth. The church opposes abortion generally because it seems to be an easy way for young people to avoid pregnancy. And while we have not taken the unyielding attitude of some other churches toward artificial birth control, we cannot officially endorse it because too many young people would stop having children. Even so, I think we will one day have to modify our position.

While working with the various marital questions, I encountered several other difficult decisions. For example, a man and a woman marry and then the man goes to war but is killed without first having any children. The woman later falls in love. She wants to be married in the temple again but is officially sealed to her first husband. Should I advise her to be sealed to the second man, which would require a cancellation of the first sealing, or should she remain sealed to her first husband, who would have claim in the hereafter on all the children of the second marriage? I was never able, in these situations, to forbid a young woman a temple cancellation so that she could marry another man and raise a family by him. Several times, when I would make my recommendations to President McKay, I would advise him, "I think we should leave it to the Lord and let him settle it and not try to settle it here." President McKay usually agreed, and even permitted several women to be sealed to two men, saying, "Let the Lord straighten it out when they get to the other side."

I look upon the question of conditions in the next world in the light of my conviction that God is all wise and that he will do for us what is for our best good. Relying on his love, wisdom, and power, I do not think we need worry much about what is going to happen when we get there. The details of life after death leave much to the imagination and to speculation.

The overall question of the eternal family goes in both directions. It is eternal backward as well as forward. There are some breaks in the line as we go back and some breaks as we go forward, but the eternity of the marriage covenant, as I grow older, becomes more and more impressive. I find that my love for my wife is greater now than it was sixty years ago when I married her. She has been a great influence in my life—all through my life.

Besides working with couples experiencing marital problems, I was assigned as an assistant to the Twelve Apostles to help lay the cornerstone of the New Zealand Temple on 22 December 1956. President McKay called me in and said, "You have been so completely wrapped up in the work you have been doing for me that I think you need a change. You need a rest. I am going to ask you to go to New Zealand and lay the cornerstone of that temple."

I went to New Zealand feeling that I had been commissioned for a special duty. I was treated during that assignment as the direct representative of the president of the church. I had never laid a cornerstone before. I had to play it by ear, but all of us seemed to get along well. I never felt more strongly the impressions of the Holy Spirit than I did on that occasion. It was a landmark in my life.

All throughout the time I served as an assistant to the Twelve, President McKay and I were very close. I could go to him at any time. He would ask me to come in and sit down and talk with him man to man. I was also close during this period to Elders Harold B. Lee, Marion G. Romney, Richard L. Evans, and Howard W. Hunter.

CHAPTER 8

A GENERAL AUTHORITY

The few years I spent as an assistant to the Quorum of the Twelve Apostles were some of the most profitable of my life. The one lesson I tried most to learn was humility.

When one is out speaking, representing the church, he is eulogized — almost idolized. What he says is taken as gospel, what he does is seen as an example to all. It places one, in other words, in the spotlight, makes one feel he is in a fishbowl and is looked upon by all who pass. Sometimes men in such positions are inclined to think that they themselves are the object of this adulation when, in fact, what people are doing is indicating their respect for the authority of the office and the appointment one has received. If we can keep in mind this fact and never abrogate to ourselves the honor which belongs to the office, we will be safe.

Unfortunately, my own experience has been that a number of the brethren never learned this lesson, instead becoming proud of the fact that they received an appointment which seemed to entitle them to the adulation of people. Sometimes they even gave evidence of the feeling that they, not their office, formed the object of an adulation which, in my opinion, should be reserved to deity.

Of course, the matter of differences of opinion is inherent in any society where people have freedom to speak their thoughts independently on religious matters. But the man who is to be successful as a church leader must learn that he is fallible, that he is mortal, and that the adulation of people can be detrimental if it gives him a wrong estimate of his own importance. Personally, I have always felt that applause is a dangerous thing to most people, even to those who may be deserving of it.

With respect to people feeling that whatever the brethren say is gospel, this tends to undermine the proposition of freedom of speech and thought. As members of the church we are bound to sustain and support the brethren in the positions they occupy so long as their conduct entitles them to that. But we also have only to defend those doctrines of the church contained in the four standard works—the Bible, the Book of Mormon, the Doctrine and Covenants, and the Pearl of Great Price. Anything beyond that by anyone is his or her own opinion and not scripture. Although there are certain statements that whatever the brethren say becomes the word of God, this is a dangerous practice to apply to all leaders and all cases. The only way I know of by which the teachings of any person or group may become binding upon the church is if the teachings have been reviewed by all the brethren, submitted to the highest councils of the church, and then approved by the whole body of the church.

I am afraid, however, that this is not as generally accepted or followed today as it ought to be. Some of the brethren have been willing to submit to the inference that what they have said was pronounced under the influence of the inspiration of the Lord and that it therefore was the will of the Lord. I do not doubt that the brethren have often spoken under inspiration and given new emphasis— perhaps even a new explanation or interpretation— of church doctrine, but that does not become binding upon the church unless and until it is submitted to the scrutiny of the rest of the brethren and later to the vote of the people. Again, we are only bound by the four standard works and are not required to defend what any man or woman says outside of them.

Official statements of the First Presidency that have not been submitted to the membership of the church for its approval are matters of temporary policy only. Under present conditions, for example, the First Presidency may say, "We recommend this or that." But conditions may subsequently change, and when they do the First Presidency may wish to make a statement which may not be in complete harmony with a former statement. We have to keep our theology up to date by submitting everything that is intended to become a permanent part of the gospel to those whose right and privilege it is to so interpret and then by having it sustained by the people as a definite rule of the church so that all things may be done by common consent.

There was a time when the Prophet Joseph Smith would ask the Lord, receive an answer, and then put the response into practice. But after the foundation of the church was laid, and its doctrinal policies established, it seemed that continued revelation of that kind would result in such a massive collection of records that nobody could tell what the law was. So we now stand upon those first, fundamental revelations. When a question arises today, we work over the details and come up with an idea. It is submitted to the First Presidency and Twelve, thrashed out, discussed and rediscussed until it seems right. Then, kneeling together in a circle in the temple, they seek divine guidance and the president says, "I feel to say this is the will of the Lord." That becomes a revelation. It is usually not thought necessary to publish or proclaim it as such, but this is the way it happens.

The heads of the church, both in the Quorum of the Twelve and in the First Presidency, are careful to see to it that none of them should ever be guilty of actions which would require discipline if they were committed by men in lower positions. For example, if I go to a stake and find a stake president who does not use his counselors but who insists on having his own way in everything and if I can not get him to reform, I release him, because the whole genius of Mormonism is cooperative action. Every man in a position of trust and authority in the church should treat his position with great care and realize that he is, after all, simply an agent — one of many — and that his personal conduct should warrant the same kind of disciplinary action that would be imposed on those working under him.

Those in high positions should guard against ever being deceived by the thought that because of their position they would be forgiven for doing things that they would not forgive others for doing. One man, who was a member of the Twelve, took it upon himself, ostensibly under the guise of polygamy, to have intimate relations with a woman other than his wife and was finally excommunicated for it. (Sometimes I think that the inspiration of many of today's polygamists comes from below the waist.)

We cannot be too careful, after being appointed to an office, about feeling that we are now somehow above the law. The fundamental principle of church government is that we govern ourselves. And unless a church leader can get rid of the temptations of life and overcome them, unless he can so order his life that others can with safety follow his example, he is not worthy to be in a high position in the church. I do not mean to intimate that a man would have to be perfect to be a General Authority of the church. But he should always be moving toward perfection, curbing his natural desires, his weaknesses, and tendencies toward self-aggrandizement and be worthy of the companionship of the Holy Spirit.

Not quite five years after I was called as an assistant to the Twelve, a vacancy arose in the Quorum of the Twelve Apostles. Nothing was said to me about it until after one of the morning sessions of General Conference when President McKay commented to me, "I would like to see you in the office here in the Tabernacle immediately at the close of this meeting." I went into the room and met with President McKay.

"The Lord wants you to be a member of the Council of the Twelve. How do you feel about it?" President McKay asked.

"If ever I was justified in criticizing what the Lord wants, I am in that position now," I answered, "because I feel that I am unprepared."

"We don't agree with you," he replied. "We have submitted your name to the Twelve and they have approved. Now what we want you to tell us is whether you will accept it."

"Of course," I said, "I will accept any call that comes from the Lord and do the best I can with it. But as for being qualified for it, I have serious doubts."

President McKay thereupon called those of the Twelve who were present in the room to join him. They surrounded me, laid their hands upon my head, and ordained me an apostle. Later, the president gave me what is known as the "charge to the apostles." That charge included a commitment to give all that one has, both as to time and means, to the building of the Kingdom of God; to keep himself pure and unspotted from the sins of the world; to be obedient to the authorities of the church; and to exercise the freedom to speak his mind but always be willing to subjugate his own thoughts and accept the majority opinion— not only to vote for it but to act as though it were his own original opinion after it has been approved by the majority of the Council of the Twelve and the First Presidency.

After they set me apart, the matter was submitted to the General Conference of the church and I was asked to say something. I spoke for only two minutes, promising that the balance of my life would be spent trying to prove that the judgment of the brethren was justified. If I could do that I would feel that I was worthy of the call. Afterwards I wrote in my journal, "This calling was very humbling indeed but is in fulfillment of a life-long ambition of my beloved mother, who predicted it when I was but a boy."

Since then I have learned that in calling a new apostle the president of the church ordinarily says to the Twelve and First Presidency, "There is a vacancy in the quorum. I would like each of you to write three names on a slip of paper and submit them to me. I will look them over and we will decide, possibly on one of those you recommend. Or we may choose none of the ones you recommend. But this will give you all an opportunity to express an opinion." At the next meeting of the quorum, the president, usually aided by the First Presidency, having looked those names over, says to the brethren, "I wish to nominate XYZ to become the next member of the Council of the Twelve. Are there any remarks? If not, all in favor, raise your right hand." When the president nominates someone whose name was not submitted by the Twelve, he simply says, "I feel inspired to appoint this man to this job. All in favor raise their hands." And everybody raises their hands. President Heber J. Grant never submitted a name as far as I know without first talking it over with his counselors and then with members of the quorum. However, President McKay, at times, chose men for certain important positions on his own responsibility, phrasing his motion in such a way as to make it difficult for the rest of the brethren not to support him.

Another of the problems I remember having to deal with personally as a General Authority had to do with permitting a young man to go on a mission who had come to Salt Lake City to attend the preparatory lessons given in the mission home. While he was here it was learned that he had been guilty of conduct not consonant with his calling. Until a missionary is forgiven of this, he or she should not be sent from the mission home into the mission field. But if, on investigation, the majority of brethren feel that the missionary should go on a mission and be forgiven of what he or she has done, then the missionary goes. There are always one or two of the brethren who believe that the missionary should not go, that his or her act makes it impossible for him or her to represent the church. I always took the other view, that if one is truly repentant, has forsaken his or her sin, done everything to make amends, then he or she should go on a mission. Perhaps, in some respects, the missionary would be more on guard against future transgression than one who had never been in such a position.

This situation was discussed very forcibly in one of the meetings of the First Presidency and Twelve, some members of the Twelve taking the position that it was wrong to let this particular missionary go. On this occasion, I took the position, inasmuch as President McKay was not present, that the case should be referred to him for decision. I was appointed by the Twelve to take it to the president, which I did. He agreed with me that the young man should be permitted to go. He went and filled a good mission, although some of the Twelve failed to forgive him.

Likewise I believe that the First Presidency should not make major decisions without submitting them to and being approved by the majority of the Twelve. I have seen this tested a number of times and am convinced that it is the best policy. I also believe that the president of the church would be well advised never to make a decision or an appointment without submitting it to the First Presidency and the Twelve. President Heber J. Grant once gave me a fine example of how inspiration sometimes prevails over personal judgment. He said that when he was a member of the Twelve and a vacancy would arise, he would write down the name of a particular boyhood friend. They had gone to school together. President Grant explained, "I knew him to be an exemplary and fine man in every respect, and I decided if I ever became president of the church he would be the first man I would appoint to the Twelve."

After he became church president and a vacancy arose in the Twelve, he wrote down the name of his friend on a slip of paper and put it into his pocket. "I went into the elevator and rode up to the fourth floor of the temple. On the way up I heard three times, as clearly as I ever heard any voice in my life, the name Melvin J. Ballard. I only knew Brother Ballard in passing, that he was at the time president of the Northwestern States Mission. But I couldn't get away from that statement and didn't give it its proper interpretation until I got into the room where the Twelve were, when I said, 'Brethren, I have decided to recommend to you a certain man to be a member of the Council of the Twelve. The man's name is . . . Melvin J. Ballard.' I know that that was inspired of the Lord," President Grant concluded.

As a General Authority I have been reversed on a number of things and have seen others appointed without the usual procedure.

A serious problem that has confronted us especially during the past few decades has been our denying the priesthood to the Negro. Personally, I doubt if we can maintain or sustain ourselves in the position we seem to have adopted but which has no justification in the scriptures, as far as I know. The president says it can only come by revelation. If that is true, then a change will come in due course. It seems to me that if we had admitted the Negro to the church as a full member at the time of the Prophet Joseph Smith, we would have had more trouble with the government than we then had. Holding ourselves aloof from that until after the Civil War gave us an opportunity to establish the church without having that question come to the front. It was, in other words, a policy, not necessarily a doctrine. [Editor's note: This policy was officially reversed by church president Spencer W. Kimball on 9 June 1978.]

The gospel of Jesus Christ teaches the universality of God's concern for all men and women and that obedience is a universal fundamental law of progress, both temporal and spiritual. The aristocracy of righteousness is the only aristocracy which God recognizes. This leaves no room for self-righteous expressions in words or actions of being "holier than thou." There is a real unity in the human race, and all men have a right to equal consideration as human beings regardless of race, creed, or color.

For any church, country, nation, or other group to believe that it is the only people in whom God is interested or that it has special merit because of color, race, or belief, that they are inherently superior and loved by God without regard to the lives they live is not only a great and dangerous fallacy but is a continuing barrier to peace. This is demoralizing, whether it is the exploded and presumptuous myth of an Aryan race of supermen or disguised in more subtle forms. We should all steadfastly avoid such demoralizing arrogance.

Another of the chief problems the brethren have to confront is what action, if any, should be taken on political questions that arise from time to time. It has been definitely established that this is a two-party church, that membership in either party does not affect one's standing in the church. For the church to take a position on a political issue is a dangerous thing because of the fact that we sustain the two-party system. I think there has been and is now too much of a tendency to cater to the wishes and decisions of one party as against the other. This must be changed.

The degree of one's aversion to Communism, for example, may not always be measured by the noise he or she makes in going about and calling everyone a communist who disagrees with his or her personal political bias. To accuse unjustifiably those who hold office of being soft on Communism is to undermine our form of government. Chapels and meeting houses should never be made available to those who seek political advantage or financial gain under the guise of fighting Communism. We must beware of groups which attack the integrity and impugn the motives of some of our greatest patriots. None of us should ever be deceived into accepting un-American and un-democratic philosophies because they bear some anti-Communist banners.

Because this is a worldwide church, we must also not be put in a public position of favoring one political philosophy over another. If the majority of citizens in a foreign country vote for a socialist government, we, as a church, should not do anything that would reflect adversely on that country's political system. The church and its leaders must not be perceived as extremist.

Every person is entitled to his or her opinion, which will be respected as long as he or she respects the opinions of others. Individual General Authorities have the right and privilege to express their own opinions, which, when expressed, represent *their* opinions only. There may be different opinions among the General Authorities, but we are united on the basic principles of the gospel. When it comes to expressing an opinion on some other organization or some political or quasi-political question, one hopes that the authorities of the church will have the good grace not to be extreme, to keep near the center of the road. All my life I have advocated that people in and out of the church should think through every proposition presented to them. Positions may be modified as time passes by discussing them with others, but there should be no question that both liberals and conservatives in the church are free to express their opinions.

When I was called into the First Presidency, President McKay greatly surprised me because I knew that the presidency was already filled. President McKay explained that I would be a counselor *to* not *in* the First Presidency. I said, "Of course, if that is the calling I will try to do the best I can." President J. Reuben Clark, President McKay's first counselor, was in ill health and could not attend many of the meetings of the First Presidency. President McKay needed help, so he called me in and said, "I'll present your name to the Twelve at their next meeting." He did and it was unanimously approved.

I went to see President Clark the very day it happened and told him that I had nothing to do with the new development but that I was simply asked to come in and help. He seemed to feel very good about it. He wept like the dickens at the time. Previously, President Clark had been severely tried by the fact that President McKay was making a number of decisions without referring to him in any way. That hurt him. He felt that his advice should have at least been sought. Although anything I may say about this change could be construed as a criticism of President

McKay, I have not always agreed with the way he dealt with President Clark's failing health. At the time, however, I wrote in my journal, "Inasmuch as the call came from the president of the church, I had but one course to take and that was to humbly accept the responsibility."

After President Clark died in 1961, I was made second counselor and President Henry D. Moyle, who had been second counselor, was made first counselor. President Moyle and I worked together with considerable harmony, although he was a one-man show and very self-confident. He had been financially and professionally successful, and, because of some of the things he said to me at times, I think in his heart he felt that I was somewhat of an upstart. But he and I were very fond of each other, and the last meeting I had with him was just inside my office door. He came in to tell me goodbye as he was leaving for Florida. With tears in his eyes, he said, "Goodbye, Hugh, we don't know for how long." He seemed to have a presentiment that he would be leaving us. He died in 1963. I was then made first counselor and my nephew, Nathan Eldon Tanner, was appointed second counselor. President McKay died in January 1970. Joseph Fielding Smith was sustained as the new president of the church. He selected Harold B. Lee as his first counselor and Nathan Eldon Tanner as second counselor. I therefore took my place in the Twelve; because of illness I have been somewhat inactive.

Although my own experiences thus far have sometimes been trying and difficult, I think there has been a purpose in all of them. As far as I am concerned, it has probably been good to have something always pestering me. It keeps me perked up. For no matter how hard we work or whatever sacrifices we may make, we are all subjected to disappointment, heartache, and sometimes despair. Both President Moyle and President Clark suffered some heartache toward the end of their lives. With the help of the Lord, however, I am not going to let that happen to me. I am going to take what comes as part of my portion in life and be satisfied with it.

If a person can come to a position where he or she is still learning, even at my age, there is reason enough to continue living. During the last ten years I have thought that each year would be my last. But this was not so ordained, and I am grateful, for I have learned many things during the last two years, things by meditation and contemplation.

As I have sat beside the bed of my wife, Zina, who is sorely afflicted by reason of a stroke, and have seen her gradually decline, I have tried to match my own accomplishments and my own weaknesses with hers, and, not wishing to be sentimental or emotional, I think the greatest person I have ever known is my wife. For some unknown reason the Lord has permitted me to live with an angel for sixty years, and I am sure that the last two years have been beneficial to me in that I have mellowed and tempered myself. I have been able to control my temper better. Recently there have been times when, in contact with the president of the church, I could have lost my temper and said things for which I would never have been entirely forgiven. Largely because of my wife's influence, I have fortunately learned to hold my temper and curb my tongue and have come away a better man. I have no bitterness, no blame, no remorse, since I believe I have done the best I could under the circumstances.

In my own life I have questioned all the things that men and women question and have had my own struggle with some problems. But I have found it desirable to lay aside some things that I do not fully understand and await the time when I will grow up enough to see them more clearly. There is so much that is good and true that I can and do approve and accept with all my heart that I can afford to wait for further light on some of these disturbing questions.

This, I think, is the purpose of life after all: to bring ourselves to a point where we can meet the vicissitudes of life in such a way as to be proud of the decisions we make, confident of the fact that we have been divinely inspired and grateful that we have been forgiven of our sins. Not in the sense that sins were never committed, but that an all-wise, merciful father, taking all things into consideration, has seen fit to forgive all of us, especially, may I add, me. I thank God that when I am judged, it shall be by one who understands me, who knows what struggles I have had to undergo and that because of this understanding, I will be shown mercy. I thank him that, though I may sometimes fall, when I go to him he will be waiting for me.

I hope that my wife and I can both live until the last one of us dies, so that when we go, we will go hand in hand. For I am afraid that this is the only way I will be able to get through the pearly gates, to hang on her hand and slip through on her record. Then when our children come up there, their mother will have a big harp and I, with chin whiskers, will have a banjo and we will play and march as they come, "littlest by littlest," as we used to say on Christmas mornings.

CHAPTER 9

A FINAL TESTIMONY

There seems today to be a tendency toward flippant thinking, a lack of thought. There seems to be a tendency to belittle what our fathers and mothers thought because we feel we have made some progress scientifically. We are too ready to conclude that everything from past generations is now folly and that our main duty today, as far as the past is concerned, is to get away from it.

There is not enough of the attitude of the sincere investigator among us. When we come into a new field of research that will challenge our due and honest consideration, we should be warned against coming too quickly to a conclusion, of forming a decision too hastily. We should be scientific—that is, open-minded, approaching new problems without prejudice, deferring a decision until all the facts are in.

Some say that the open-minded leave room for doubt. But I believe we should doubt some of the things we hear. Doubt has a place if it can stir in one an interest to go out and find the truth for one's self. I should like to awaken in everyone a desire to investigate, to make an independent study of religion, and to know for themselves whether or not the teachings of the Mormon church are true.

I should like to see everyone prepared to defend the religion of his or her parents, not because it was the religion of our fathers and mothers but because they have found it to be the true religion. If one approaches it with an open mind, with a desire to know the truth, and if one questions with a sincere heart what one hears from time to time, he or she will be on the road to growth and service.

There are altogether too many people in the world who are willing to accept as true whatever is printed in a book or delivered from a pulpit. Their faith never goes below the surface soil of authority. I plead with everyone I meet that they may drive their faith down through that soil and get hold of the solid truth, that they may be able to withstand the winds and storms of indecision and of doubt, of opposition and persecution. Then, and only then, will we be able to defend our religion successfully. When I speak of defending our religion, I do not mean such defense as an army makes on the battlefield but the defense of a clean and upright and virtuous life lived in harmony with an intelligent belief and understanding of the gospel. As Mormons, we should do with religion as we do with music, not defend it but simply render it. It needs no defense. The living of religion is, after all, the greatest sermon, and if all of us would live it, we would create a symphony which would be appreciated by all.

There are many churches in the world today, and in those churches are many people and many kinds of theology. I would like to distinguish between theology and religion. Religion is my preference. Someone has said, "I hate botany, but I love flowers." I would say that I do not care for theology, but I love religion.

In my travels I have found a great many people who have had some rather perverted ideas about Mormons. Frequently during my army days I was asked, "How many wives do you have?" And I would say, "Well, I live in a country where we have all the wives we want." Of course, I was immediately met with a knowing smile, and some of my army friends would comment, "I would like to live in a country like that." I would answer, "Don't you live in a country where you have all the wives you want? We have all the wives we want in Utah, but we only want one each."

The Mormon church has a religion aside from its theology, which, if followed, dominates the life of individuals and leads them up out of the gruelling surroundings which life may have placed them in, and teaches them that they are children of God and that being children of God they are of royal blood. The Church of Jesus Christ of Latter-day Saints has this practical view of religion: that religion should help us here and now; that we should not have to wait until after we are dead to get any benefits; that religion as understood and applied makes men and women more successful, happier, more contented, gives them aspiration and hope; that religion is the vitalizing force, religion is that which gives men and women an ideal, an ideal so high that it may be seen from both sides of the valley of life. The religion of the Latter-day Saints teaches youth that as children of God, they are expected to acquire experience as they go through life and that experience will ripen into knowledge, that knowledge will ripen into wisdom and intelligence, and that their greatness will be in proportion to their intelligence.

So the religion of the Latter-day Saints is not just theory from a book or taught in church. The gospel is a plan of which God is the author, a plan of which we are all necessary parts.

My religion sweetens my life. My religion, if properly lived, helps me to be a better friend to my associates, a better neighbor, a better citizen, a better father, a better man. If I am sincere in it, my religion forbids me to do to my neighbors what I would not want them to do to me, either in word or act. My religion, in other words, is that which is the greatest part of me.

I have been very grateful that the freedom, dignity, and integrity of the individual are basic in church doctrine. We are free to think and express our opinions in the church. Fear will not stifle thought. God himself refuses to trammel free agency even though its exercise sometimes teaches painful lessons. Both creative science and revealed religion find their fullest and truest expression in the climate of freedom.

As we all proceed to make our individual "declarations of independence," I hope we can all distinguish between liberty and license, that we can realize that freedom is only a blessing if it is accompanied by wisdom and intelligence. At the same time, we all need to resist the down-drag of mental laziness which sometimes leads to the premature hardening of the intellectual arteries. And I would especially urge all of us to avoid sluggishness of spirit, which is the worst kind of lethargy. Some people are phlegmatic to a degree that would make a turtle seem intolerably vivacious.

I admire men and women who have developed the questing spirit, who are unafraid of new ideas as stepping stones to progress. We should, of course, respect the opinions of others, but we should also be unafraid to dissent—if we are informed. Thoughts and expressions compete in the marketplace of thought, and in that competition truth emerges triumphant. Only error fears freedom of expression.

Both science and religion beget humility. Scientists and teachers of religion disagree among themselves on theological and other subjects. Even in our own church men and women take issue with one another and contend for their own interpretations. This free exchange of ideas is not to be deplored as long as men and women remain humble and teachable. Neither fear of consequence or any kind of coercion should ever be used to secure uniformity of thought in the church. People should express their problems and opinions and be unafraid to think without fear of ill consequences.

We should all be interested in academic research. We must go out on the research front and continue to explore the vast unknown. We should be in the forefront of learning in all fields, for revelation does not come only through the prophet of God nor only directly from heaven in visions or dreams. Revelation may come in the laboratory, out of the test tube, out of the thinking mind and the inquiring soul, out of search and research and prayer and inspiration. We must be unafraid to contend for what we are thinking and to combat error with truth in this divided and imperiled world, and we must do it with the unfaltering faith that God is still in his heaven even though all is not well with the world.

We should be dauntless in our pursuit of truth and resist all demands for unthinking conformity. No one would have us become mere tape recorders of other people's thoughts. We should be modest and teachable and seek to know the truth by study and faith. There have been times when progress was halted by thought control. Tolerance and truth demand that all be heard and that competing ideas be tested against each other so that the best, which might not always be our own, can prevail. Knowledge is most complete and dependable when all points of view are heard. We are in a world of restlessness and skepticism, where old things are not only challenged but often disappear, but also a world of miraculous achievement, undreamed of accomplishment, and terrifying power.

Science offers wonderful tools for helping to create the brotherhood of humanity on earth, but the cement of brotherhood does not come from any laboratory. It must come from the heart and mind and spirit of men and women.

Peace and brotherhood can be achieved when the two most potent forces in civilization—religion and science—join to create one world in its truest and greatest sense. We should continue to become acquainted with human experience through history and philosophy, science and poetry, art and religion. Every discovery of science reveals clearly the divine plan in nature. The remarkable harmony in the physical laws and processes of the universe, from the infinitesimal to the infinite, surpasses mortal understanding and implies a supreme architect, and the beauty and symmetry of God's handiwork inspire reverence.

One of the most important things in the world is freedom of the mind; from this all other freedoms spring. Such freedom is necessarily dangerous, for one cannot think right without running the risk of thinking wrong, but generally more thinking is the antidote for the evils that spring from wrong thinking.

More thinking is required, and we should all exercise our God-given right to think and be unafraid to express our opinions, with proper respect for those to whom we talk and proper acknowledgment of our own shortcomings. We must preserve freedom of the mind in the church and resist all efforts to suppress it. The church is not so much concerned with whether the thoughts of its members are orthodox or heterodox as it is that they shall have thoughts. One may memorize much without learning anything. In this age of speed there seems to be little time for meditation.

While I speak of independence and the right to think, to agree or disagree, to examine and question, I need to remind myself not to forget that fixed and unchanging laws govern all God's creation, whether the vastness of the starry heavens or the minute revolving universe of the atom or human relationships. All is law. All is cause and effect, and God's laws are universal. God has no favorites; no one is immune from either life's temptations or the consequences of his or her deeds. God is not capricious.

An individual's reactions to the ever-changing impacts of life will depend upon his or her goals and ideals. Every life revolves around certain fundamental core ideas, whether we realize it or not, and herein lies the chief value of religion. But while I believe *all* that God has revealed, I am not quite sure I understand *what* he has revealed, and the fact that God has promised further revelation is to me a challenge to keep an open mind and be prepared to follow wherever my search for truth may lead.

We Mormons have been blessed with much knowledge by revelation from God which, in some part, the world lacks. But there is an incomprehensibly greater part of truth yet to be discovered. Revealed insights should leave us stricken with the knowledge of how little we really know. It should never lead to an emotional arrogance based upon a false assumption that we somehow have all the answers—that we in fact have a corner on truth. For we do not.

And while all members should respect, support, and heed the teachings of the authorities of the church, no one should accept a statement and base his or her testimony upon it, no matter who makes it, until he or she has, under mature examination, found it to be true and worthwhile; then one's logical deductions may be confirmed by the spirit of revelation to his or her spirit, because real conversion must come from within.

I hope that the spirit of the Holy Ghost rests upon everyone and leads us all back into the presence of our heavenly parents. I hope that everyone might conduct his or her life in such a manner as to be worthy of God's continued blessings. And I especially hope that we might all be able, as we go forward, to walk figuratively and almost literally with our hand in God's hand and to feel the effect of God's presence in our lives, doing everything in Jesus' name and with God's blessings.

EDITOR'S AFTERWORD

By the time Grandfather and I completed our taping sessions in late 1970, President David O. McKay had died and Grandfather would live only for an additional five years. Through years of shared service in the church, especially as members of the First Presidency, President McKay and Grandfather had become loving, intimate friends. This was not always the case, at least to that degree. For while I know of no antagonism between them in earlier years, both had similar strengths and weaknesses. Both were tall, patrician, handsome men; both were gifted orators and were in demand as speakers; and both could be proud as well as humble. I believe an understandable sense of competition existed between them in earlier years.

But during Grandfather's years as a third counselor to President McKay (when President J. Reuben Clark's health was failing) and then as second counselor (with Henry D. Moyle) and later first counselor (with N. Eldon Tanner), a very warm and intimate bond of love formed between the two men—the kind that can only grow when people finally move beyond self-seeking. During these years of good health, President McKay told Grandfather on a number of occasions that he was happier and more satisfied with the loving unity of the First Presidency than at any time in his presidency.

The period when President McKay's health began to decline was another matter. This was a difficult time in church government, but it also marked one of Grandfather's greatest periods of service. As President McKay became increasingly impaired by age, some church functionaries, with allegiances to the radical political right, tried to influence the president in ways that Grandfather, President Tanner, and Elder Harold B. Lee thought unwise and improper. These three men—Grandfather in particular—were

141

often but not always successful in blocking those efforts to influence church policy. This effort took a fearful toll on Grandfather, both physically and in his personal relationships.

Theologically, Grandfather had tried for years to effect a change in the Mormon policy that denied the priesthood to blacks. As he explained in his memoirs, he never believed this policy had the slightest doctrinal justification, and he succeeded in initiating a number of administrative changes to mitigate the effects of this ban. He changed the way racial heritage was determined, which smoothed the way to priesthood ordination for thousands of people in nations such as Brazil. With President McKay's support he also attempted to open an African mission. But this plan ultimately failed.

Grandfather was eventually able to get a proposal allowing full priesthood for blacks approved by the Quorum of the Twelve Apostles. Elder Harold B. Lee was not present when this proposal was approved, and because of the advanced age of Joseph Fielding Smith, then president of the Quorum of the Twelve, Elder Lee was the dominant senior voice among the Twelve. Convinced that the ban was doctrinally based, Elder Lee sought to memorialize his belief by drafting a statement on the matter for the First Presidency's consideration. At the time, President McKay's health was failing and he did not sign such documents. Grandfather managed to add language to Elder Lee's statement endorsing full civil rights for all citizens, but he still resisted signing the statement. However, he suffered from advanced age and the late stages of Parkinson's disease and was ill with the Asian flu. With Grandfather in this condition, Elder Lee brought tremendous pressure to bear upon him, arguing that with President McKay incapacitated Grandfather was obliged to join the consensus within the Quorum of the Twelve. Grandfather, deeply ill, wept as he related this story to me just before he signed the statement that bore his and President Tanner's names.

Grandfather was dropped from the First Presidency when it was reorganized under Joseph Fielding Smith in 1970. Although his health was declining, Grandfather did not believe this was the reason for his return to the Quorum of Twelve Apostles. I believe without the slightest doubt that his position on blacks and the priesthood was the matter that led to his removal from the new First Presidency. This policy change on blacks — so vital in freeing all our souls — would come several years later during the presidency of Spencer W. Kimball, a man Grandfather loved dearly. By then all the major protagonists in the earlier struggle would have already died: Harold B. Lee, Joseph Fielding Smith, and Grandfather.

Grandfather came to believe that the church was not sufficiently addressing the problem of age and infirmity in its leadership. In an attempt to meet this need, after his return to the Twelve, he proposed that an emeritus status be created for all General Authorities, including members of the Quorum of the Twelve and the First Presidency. This would have affected the line of succession to the presidency of the church. His proposal deliberately set the age for emeritus status so that he would have been rendered emeritus by adoption of his plan. He told me, only half in jest, that getting rid of him should have sweetened the proposal for at least some quorum members. His proposal was rejected, but under President Kimball a truncated version was later adopted for authorities at less important levels of church government.

Although I personally believe we as a church were poorer without Grandfather and his sensitivity on social and moral issues in the First Presidency, Grandfather's final years of service in the Quorum was a sweet time of final service. He toured missions, visited stakes, and preached with profound eloquence. He touched souls as few are able to do.

Happily, during these last years, he and Harold B. Lee became reconciled. The two had been dear friends long before they were General Authorities. At one point after his return to the Twelve, Grandfather became gravely ill and was not expected to live through the night. His daughters, Zina and Mary, and I were summoned that night by the doctor. Brother Lee, by now president of the church, joined the family, and we prepared a press release announcing his death. We blessed and anointed Grandfather, and President Lee spoke words of reconciliation in a blessing that brought Grandfather momentarily out of his coma into tearful consciousness. The next morning he awoke, looked the doctor in the eye, and said, characteristically, "I fooled you, didn't I!" Grandfather lived for several more years, although President Lee died soon thereafter.

Grandfather's and Grandmother's final years of life together were bittersweet. Grandmother lived through a massive stroke in August 1966 and then several smaller strokes which left her an invalid, unable to leave her bed or to talk. I lived virtually next door to them at the time. Grandfather, his legs beginning to fail although his mind was as alert as ever, would try to exercise. With a cane, his upper body seeming to move dangerously faster than his legs, he would pass our window, wave, go to the end of the street and return to Grandmother's side. As I watched him, I remembered a poignant moment in the early 1960s when Grandfather had taken me to meet J. Reuben Clark prior to his death. As we were leaving, Grandfather said tenderly, "Is there any- thing we can do for you, Reuben?" Brother Clark started to cry. He said, "Pray for me, Hugh, that I can endure to the end." They embraced and we left. Now it was Grandfather's and Grandmother's turn.

Grandmother lay in bed for nearly eight years, fully conscious most of the time and completely unable to serve herself in any way. For decades Grandmother had served Grandfather quietly and, as far as the world was concerned, invisibly. Now he, with the help of his children and nurses, had the chance to serve her. He did so joyously. So far as I saw and heard, there was not a complaint from either of them to God or to anyone else. Return- ing from a church assignment, he would approach what had been the dining room—an airy, light room at the front of the house now converted for Grandmother's use. Always with a flower, he would tap on her window and say, with an accent learned from over a decade of church service in his beloved England, "Toot, toot, Mama! I'm here! Your sweetheart is home." Then he would hobble in with a cane in one hand and the arm of a son or daugh- ter or grandchild in the other and greet his mate of over sixty years.

Grandfather was the only one, doctors and children not excepted, who could bring Grandmother instantly out of the deepest coma. On several occasions I saw him stand over her bed and say simply, "Zina." She would awake immediately, open her eyes, and smile. He asked her not to die before he did, and she made a valiant effort to comply. Grandmother died in December 1974, and Grandfather followed almost exactly one year later.

Grandfather was an infinitely curious man. He had a wanderlust that took him to almost every part of the globe. Suffering from a crippling disease and in his nineties, he wanted to plan a trip to China or Russia for the two of us, the only places he had not visited. He read voraciously, primarily history, biography, politics, philosophy, and religion. Even as a young boy, I had been drawn to his huge library, borrowing books we both knew I would never return. Once, near the end, he called me and said, "Eddie, I haven't received the last issue of *Dialogue [A Journal of Mormon Thought]*. Do you think they've cut me off from the church?" I assured him that they would not do that. He asked that I call to make sure his subscription had not lapsed.

He approached death with the same curiosity with which he approached life. He instructed us that no heroic measures were to be used to prolong his life and particularly that he be given no drugs that would dull his sensory experience of death. He told me that he was likely to enjoy this only once, and he did not want to miss a thing. Never once did he speak fearfully or regretfully or disparagingly of death. He loved life and enjoyed it enormously. But he also anticipated death with what I can only describe as positive zest. We speculated together about the nature of life after death. He had absolutely no doubt about our continuing to live. In fact, he promised, only half jokingly, to come back and tell me what is was like. He has not done that yet, and I still hold him to the promise.

Near the end, Grandfather dreamed of dear friends who had preceded him in death: Stayner Richards, Marvin O. Ashton, Harold B. Lee. One night he dreamed he was in the Savior's presence. No words were exchanged. He said none were necessary. "His love enriched me, and I felt his understanding acceptance of me despite all my imperfect ways." He wept as he related the dream.

As he approached death, confined to bed or at best a wheelchair, he endured the humiliation of incontinence with wistful humor. He had to be fed as well. Even then, when his powerful magnifying glass would no longer allow him to read, he asked that we read to him. The morning following a mild stroke that caused a slurring of his speech, he asked that we read him the morning paper. He frowned at the dourness of the day's news. Then he indicated that we should read the obituary page. He asked if his name was there and, when assured that it was not, slurred the words, "Son of obituary!"

Though quite infirm, he wanted desperately to attend the dedication of the Washington, D.C., Temple in late 1974. He had been instrumental in selecting the temple's site, conducted its ground breaking ceremony, and was involved in seeing it to completion. Solicitous friends made arrangements for Grandfather to be flown to Washington and to have Dr. Russell Nelson in the room next to him.

Although an office was maintained for him at church headquarters, he conducted almost all of his business at home during these final years. His daughter Zina devoted almost her full time to assisting her parents. Grandfather died on 2 December 1975 in the LDS hospital with Zina holding his hand.

Grandfather believed devoutly in the gospel of Jesus Christ and possessed a profound testimony of Joseph Smith's restoration. Yet he refused to accept those lines by which we divide ourselves from each other, whether within religion or politics. He had broad and loving contact, as did President Grant and President McKay before him, with religious leaders of other faiths. By his very nature, his own resonant psychology and spirituality, Grandfather possessed an ecumenical spirit.

In politics, as Grandfather repeatedly expressed in his memoirs, he was an ardent Democrat. As a young boy growing up in a Republican family and vaguely aware that most church leaders were Republicans, I asked Grandfather why he was a Democrat. "Eddie," he said, "I'm a Democrat because I believe that party is more sensitive to the poor." His answer seemed to me simplistic at the time. But since then it has impressed me as a good criterion by which to judge both politics and religion.

Grandfather left a rich legacy to his family and to the church. He touched thousands of lives intimately, giving of himself without restraint.

Few speakers of his generation approached his eloquence, his fervor in preaching the gospel of Jesus Christ. He will not be remembered as a great theologian. But anyone who heard his voice or saw and felt his commanding presence was moved by what they experienced. He had the capacity to help men and women change their lives.

He possessed great spiritual and intellectual honesty and refused to be limited by those who tried to read others out of orthodoxy. Grandfather felt that we were all forbidden to exercise this judgment against ourselves or others. He gloried in intellectual and spiritual freedom, which, he said, were consistent with the Mormon teaching of agency and the eternal nature of human intelligence: "When I consult my own inner self, I find a deep-seated, perhaps instinctive feeling of immeasurable oldness, an echo of time immemorial, as well as a feeling of necessary endlessness. No adverse logic or reason can dispel these feelings. I did not put them there, I found them there. When I grew old enough to introspect my mind, and in spite of recurrent doubts and criticism, this innate knowledge has remained unimpaired."

He appreciated fully Joseph Smith's refusal to adopt rigid creeds which presume to define God and our relationship to him. He defined the gospel as encompassing all knowledge and refused to assign more truth to scripture or to any other prophetic teaching than he assigned to the traces of God's finger which he saw in the stones of the earth, the stars of the cosmos, and the center of our own souls. He recognized obedience to authority as a virtue, but he placed more value on fidelity to God, discipleship to Jesus, and a loving relationship with others. He realized that his responsibility for his own acts could never be borne by another, leader or not.

Truly he possessed a universal, Pauline spirit that pushes to the widest possible limits the Thirteenth Article of Faith of the Mormon church: "We believe all things, we hope all things, we have endured many things, and hope to be able to endure all

147

things. If there is anything virtuous, lovely, or of good report or praiseworthy, we seek after these things."

We miss him.

INDEX